A Witch's Mirror
The Art of Making Magic

By
Levannah Morgan

GW00630641

www.capallbann.co.uk

A Witch's Mirror

©Copyright 2013 Levannah Morgan

ISBN 1861633467
ISBN 13 978186163 3460

Cover design by HR Print and Design Ltd
Cover and internal illustrations by Lee Noble

Published by:

Capall Bann Publishing
Auton Farm
Milverton
Somerset
TA4 1NE

For Emma

Acknowledgments

To Hereward Wake and Cecil Williamson who taught me much of my craft I owe eternal thanks. Hail to their spirits!

Special thanks to all the members of the Coven of the Silver Wheel, past and present, who have worked this magic with me, and accompanied me on countless adventures, especially Emma, Jemma, Ian, Elayne, Deborah, Julian, Trudie, Louise, Ronald, Andrea and Clare. Also to Rob, Jan, Vivianne, Chris, Jean and Jim for wise advice and guidance. I would also like to thank Graham King, Kerriann Godwin, Joyce Froome and Hannah Fox at the Museum of Witchcraft, Boscastle, Cornwall for wonderful discussions of magic and witchcraft and for access to their superb collections and archives.

Thanks to Jon and Julia at Capall Bann for all their encouragement and support.

Most of all I would like to thank my beloved husband Lee not only for his illustrations for this book, but also for his patience, help and understanding during the writing of it.

Levannah Morgan, Devon 2012

Contents

Introduction

What is witchcraft? Witchcraft is worshipping the Old Gods on a moonlit night on a high tor on Dartmoor. Witchcraft is tying nine knots in a red thread. Witchcraft is walking in the spirit world. Witchcraft is catching the moon in a mirror. Witchcraft is collecting rowan berries. Witchcraft is living with familiar spirits. Witchcraft is making a circle of holed stones. Witchcraft is dancing with the Horned God. Witchcraft is sitting on a deserted beach as the tides ebb and flow. Witchcraft is the oldest thing there is. Witchcraft is making magic. Witchcraft is all of these things and much more.

This is a book about practical witchcraft and magic-making. I have been working as a witch for over thirty years and for most of that time I have lived in Devon, in the south west of England. Devon is a county with a wealth of magical traditions which are still observed in some of the more rural areas. The place in which I live has shaped my witchcraft over the years and made it what it is.

For me, witchcraft is a timeless activity which has been practised in all times and in all places. We can see and instinctively recognise the practice of magic in the art and artefacts left behind by the earliest humans. Most witches in the west today are also Pagans but over the years I have met witches working within many different spiritual traditions, including Islam and Christianity, so I have learnt not to be prescriptive. Witchcraft may take different forms according to when and where it is practised, but at its heart is always the desire and ability to make magic and work with the spirits, seen and unseen that surround us.

I grew up in a remote rural area in the late 1950s and early 1960s where there was no television and many of the contrivances and conveniences of the modern world were absent. Few people had telephones, the internet had not been invented, and most people did not travel much but lived all their lives in the place where they had been born. In the absence of these things, it was taken for granted that gods and spirits were present amongst us, and that stones, trees and water had their own indwelling guardian spirits which had to be honoured and respected. If the spirits were properly honoured, people, homes, land and animals would be kept safe and well and I was taught how to do this from an early age. Certain trees, rocks and springs would always be spoken to and properly acknowledged. If a house was cold and unhappy, or a garden would not grow, there were people who would consult the spirits, and magic would be used to put things right.

In witchcraft, doing things, taking action and making things are as important as words. Rituals are a vital part of serving the gods, but practical and often simple, direct actions are an essential part of magic-making. Magic is something that should be lived. Much of the magic in this book is about apparently simple things, such as sitting out in a forest all day, standing in moonlight, collecting berries or pebbles, or looking at the sea in a mirror. It is my belief that these things, experienced with all the senses, and done with intent, can be deep forms of magic and have the most profound effect, and be just as powerful as complex rituals, if not more so. I hope that I can encourage you to make your own magic in many practical and heartfelt ways.

I have been fortunate to have two wonderful magical teachers. I practised witchcraft on my own for years before joining a Wiccan coven. My initiator, a wonderful man called Hereward Wake, had a lifetime's experience of both witchcraft and ritual magic which he shared generously with me. From him I learnt how to worship the gods in ritual and how to voyage into the spirit world; how to look and to listen and to work with the hidden senses; when to act and when to be still and do nothing. Cecil Williamson, who founded the Museum of Witchcraft, spent his life learning the ways of the traditional witch. He taught me about the old witchcraft that was used in Devon: spells, charms and a myriad of ways of interacting with the spirit world. My own witchcraft has grown and changed over the years; I have taken what Hereward and Cecil showed me and adapted it for my own needs. I owe both of them an immense debt of gratitude. Both of them showed me that the ultimate teachers are the gods and the spirits and that magic works because the witch is guided by them. Over the years I have passed on what I have learnt, person to person, to students of the craft and I have frequently been asked to make some of this knowledge more widely available. I hope this book will go some way towards doing this.

When I first learnt, witchcraft was a very quiet, hidden craft. There were few books available and learning was passed on by practical example from witch to witch. Teachers would lend precious handwritten journals to students for the copying of rituals and spells. It was not possible to buy readymade working tools and paraphernalia as it is now. Almost everything had to be made. Making these things was not just a matter of necessity. Tools and other objects made by the witch have a magical power all of their own. Something that has been bought inevitably has a very different feeling. Hereward Wake made everything for his coven: wands, athames, pentacles, cups and altar objects were made from materials sought out from forests, beaches and the wild places of Dartmoor and Exmoor, and the seeking out and making of magical tools and artefacts was one of the first lessons that I learnt. When Hereward retired in his late seventies, he passed the running of his coven on to me and practical magic making has always been at the heart of what the coven does. This book aims to pass on this experiential approach to witchcraft. We make our own tools, ritual clothing, incense and countless spells, charms and other magical things. None of us started out with any special craft skills but we have learnt along the way how to make things that work. Something that has a real power and presence will always work better than something that simply looks good. A visiting witch once commented jokingly that a meeting of my coven resembled an alternative Womens Institute meeting, and I have always rather cherished this description.

This is not a book of formal rituals of witchcraft. There are plenty of these available elsewhere and the form rituals take will vary according to the tradition you choose to follow. It is up to you to choose which particular deities you wish to honour and which forms of ritual you wish to celebrate. Rather, this book aims to inspire you to work your own magic through making and doing things. I hope that you will use it rather like a recipe book to create your own magic and that it will help you to develop your own ways of working. It contains simple but profound magical techniques and plenty of practical projects. All of them have been inspired by the places where I live and work, and I hope you will take them and let the spirits guide you to make your own magic. You do not need any specialist art or craft skills, just enthusiasm, dedication, and a desire to work magic. Many of the chapters overlap, and you can take techniques and projects from one subject and apply them to others as you become more confident in your magic-making.

I have written about the places I know because they are the places I know. They have formed and shaped my witchcraft; without these places it would not exist. You can practise your witchcraft wherever you live, whether in the countryside or a city. You will put down your magical roots in the places where you work and these places and their spirits will help you and teach you. You do not need lots of money to make your magic. You will find the materials you need in the world around you;

the gods and spirits will provide what is required. A walk along a beach will provide shells, stones and driftwood. In the forest you will find wood, fruits and other treasures. Jumble and car boot sales and recycling skips and tips will provide the things you need at little or no cost. This is a deliberately frugal way of working which runs counter to the consumer ethic which is so prevalent today. Witches hold Nature in great reverence. We work with what we are given, re-using and recycling, rather than wasting precious resources.

All the craft and making activities which I have described in this book are reasonably safe. Fellow witches and I have tested all of them. They are intended for adults. Please do be sensible when working with things such as sharp knives, needles, boiling jam and hot wax. Please also take only what you need when gathering natural resources, especially plants. Do not be wasteful and leave plenty for other beings.

Please *do* try this at home.

Magic

This book is about the processes of magical working, the magical attitude of mind and the wealth of small but vital activities and processes that make magic work. Magic is an elusive concept which tends to resist finite definitions. One useful starting point is the definition formulated by the magician Aleister Crowley:

" Magic is the art and science of causing change, in accordance with Will".

Like the wind; magic is hard to pin down, but we know it when we feel and experience it. People in general tend to think of magic as an act that is performed to achieve a specific objective. This is what witches refer to as operative magic; a working or a spell designed to fulfil a practical purpose. It works when the effect we seek to create is achieved. However, witches know that there is also a deeper form of magic which happens when we come into close contact with our gods or with the spirit world. This is the kind of magic which changes witches themselves, rather than the world around them. Over many centuries witches and magicians have worked with the idea that there is an essential power or energy which makes the universe work. This power has had many names in different cultures. The Egyptians called it *hekaa*, a word which is usually translated rather inadequately into English as "magic". In the east it has been known as *prana* and *chi*, and in the west it has had many different names. Deep magic means opening up oneself to this power and becoming one with it, and the witch knows in their mind, heart and bones when this has been achieved. This kind of magic may be worked through large, complex rituals, but it can equally be achieved by quiet, less dramatic activities, such as sitting out in a wood or on a beach all day, or through working seemingly small changes in one's life, such as learning to live by lunar and tidal time. Opening the self up to this power and working with it is the essence of witchcraft.

In order to work real, deep magic, the witch must develop their magical will. The will is the witch's magical mind; a finely focused combination of concentration and desire which operates at a very profound level, outside the everyday world and its concerns. Recognising the magical will and learning to work with it is vital, and not necessarily easy. I was fortunate to have wonderful teachers to guide me through this and it is the most important thing that I teach those who come to me to learn witchcraft. Working with the magical will means stilling the everyday mind through meditation and going deep inside oneself until there is nothing but the great power of the universe. When I am in touch with this power I feel a sense of very calm but focused excitement which is physical as well as mental. There is no separation between the mind and the body.

Magic, like any power, may be used for many purposes. Some traditions will only use magic for "good" purposes; others make no such distinctions. In the end, moral and ethical choices must be made by the witch themselves. There is an old saying that in order to bless, the witch must also know how to curse. If you are open about your witchcraft, people will ask you to work operative magic for them, and you will have to decide whether or not to help them. My own personal ethics are that I will not work magic for profit, or for very small things, as I believe that this devalues the great power of magic and trivialises it. I will work magic to help friends and family going through difficulties, but only if they have asked me to do so. Rushing in with magical help unbidden seems to me arrogant, and interfering with the workings of the universe. I don't work love spells for people, because I do not wish to compel someone to love another person against their will. I will work protective and banishing magic to return harm to its sender, if I genuinely think this is needed. In the end you must make decisions about these matters for yourself, but do not be tempted to trivialise magic. If you do so, you will find that your ability to work magically will suffer. Also, remember that magic may have unintended side effects, so think things through very carefully first. The old adage "be careful what you wish for" is a very true one.

The Gods

Like most contemporary witches, I honour and worship the old Pagan gods who were revered for millennia before the advent of Christianity and the other patriarchal, monotheistic religions. A fundamental part of witchcraft is the honouring of a Goddess and God. I was one of the many women who "came home" to witchcraft because it recognised that deity is female as well as male. At a profound level, witches know that it is the interaction between two great polarities, which we may describe as male/ female, yin/ yang, or light/ dark that drives the universe. Language is, of course, inadequate to describe these great forces and you will come to understand them and describe them in your own way.

I honour the Goddess of the Moon and the tides (and have written about Her in more detail in the chapters on The Moon and The Tides). Witchcraft is in many ways about working with what is hidden from the everyday, so understanding and honouring the power of the Moon and all she represents is vital for me. I also honour the Goddess as our Mother the Earth, who sustains and nourishes us.

The God of the witches is the Horned Lord, known to our forebears by many names including Cernunnos, Herne, Robin,

Janicot and sometimes just Old Hornie. Humans have made images of Him since the earliest times. He is the power of life, growth and the fertility of the world around us. He is all that grows; the Lord of the animals. He is the power behind the seasons; he is born at Midwinter and grows with the year. He is the corn and the vine which we sacrifice and cut down at the harvest, and which we eat and drink. As the year turns to winter he disappears from the earth and becomes the Dark Lord, leader of the Wild Hunt whom we see in the constellation of Orion the Hunter which becomes visible in October and is with us until the year turns to spring again.

I celebrate the monthly cycles of the moon and the solar year. Through the ceaseless round of the ever-changing seasons I mark the passage of Goddess and God around the year in a way that will be familiar to Pagans. I prefer to use the old names for the seasonal festivals rather than some of the ones that have come into use over the last thirty years as they are what I was taught and full of meaning and symbolism for me. The sun is reborn from the womb of the great Mother on Mothernight at Midwinter (21st December). At Candlemas (2nd February) I celebrate the return of the light and the Goddess as maiden of ice and fire, patroness of all the arts and of healing. At Spring Equinox (21st March) when the days become longer than the nights the God comes into his strength and seeds are planted in his honour. At Mayday (1st May) growth is at its peak and the mystical marriage of Goddess and God is celebrated. At Midsummer (21st June) the God at the height of his powers dances the circle of the zodiac. At Lammas (1st August), the ancient harvest festival which has been celebrated in these islands since the stone age, the corn is cut and the God is cut down in the cornfield and gives himself for us as bread and ale. At Autumn Equinox (21st September) the God is gone from the earth and becomes the Lord of the Wild Hunt, hunting the skies with his spectral wish hounds. At this time I consider my own harvest of all that I have made, grown and learnt in the growing season and begin my interior journey through the dark months. At Halloween (31st October), the festival of the dead and the ancestors, the veil between the world of the living and that of the dead thins and we may meet and commune with the spirits of the dead. The God, the Lord of the Shadows, opens the gates between these worlds and the Goddess as Mother of the Tides presides. This is the time of great dreams and visions when we can journey deep into the dark. Then the endless round begins again at the Mothernight.

These festivals may be celebrated in different ways in different traditions, but their essential meaning is the same. The God is the solar year and the year is articulated in his growth, harvest and falling away. The Goddess has her seasonal aspects too: Maiden as the light returns and the year begins to grow, Queen and Mother when the year is at its peak, and Hag in the cold, dark months, but she is ever-present and does not pass away from the earth when winter comes as the God does. There is a subtle interplay of the great polarities of Goddess and God at each of these seasonal rites.

The Goddess is honoured continually through each lunar month (see the chapter on the Moon). Over many years, honouring Goddess and God through this yearly cycle has worked a profound change in the way I experience the seasons and the changes they bring in me and in the world around me. It means that I am very aware of the constant small changes in weather, patterns of daylight and darkness and the plants and animals around them. I see myself as part of these processes, not separate or distanced from them. It has brought an increased sensitivity to everything that happens around me, which helps me understand the world and myself better, and which I cherish. At Mayday/ Beltane, for example I am carried along by an exuberant tide of energy. Growth is at its height in all living things and I can physically sense the growth energy of the trees and other plants around me. All of this is expressed in the seasonal cycle as the wild, passionate union of Goddess and God. At Autumn Equinox I experience a peaceful, melancholic turning away from the external world as the god passes from the earth into the stars and I begin the journey of the dark months into the interior world of dreams, visions and scrying. I have come to understand and love all the changes the seasons bring and feel that I am fully part of them. This understanding of the solar year is one of the great gifts that witchcraft brings.

Honouring the Gods and working magic are for me one indivisible whole and each enriches the other. Goddess and God are invoked and preside over the practice of magic.

The Spirit World

The world is full of spirits; beings which have no physical body. Spirits are usually sensed or heard but may take on visible form. Witches believe that everything is alive and has its own spirit. Particular places have their own spirits as do rocks, trees, plants and water. The elements each have their own class of spirits: Sylphs for air, Salamanders for fire, Undines for water and Gnomes for earth. Many parts of Britain have local names for nature spirits which inhabit particular places. In Devon, the spirits of Dartmoor are known as Pixies. In Cornwall there are Piskies and Spriggans. In the North of England there are Boggarts and in Wales you may meet the Tylwyth Teg. You will doubtless recognise many of these names from children's fairy tales but be aware these spirits have been honoured for centuries and are not the gentle, harmless creatures of popular culture. You may be able to buy a cute little figure of a Dartmoor Pixie with a red pointy hat and green jacket to put in your garden, but if you ever encounter the real thing out on the Moor you will surely know about it.

The Pixies of Dartmoor like to confuse people and get them lost; this is known as being Pixie-led. Once out on the Moor with Hereward Wake and the coven we walked to a working place and worked our magic. When we came to go home we knew that the path led over a broad hill in front of us but none of us could find it. When we looked at the hill ahead we could see nothing; it disappeared into a vague whiteness which was not mist. Every step we tried to take left us confused and discombobulated. Hereward had the answer: we were being Pixie-led. He made us take the traditional remedy which is to turn one's clothes inside out. We stopped and honoured the Pixies and put our coats on inside out. Instantly the path appeared again, the feelings of doubt and confusion vanished, and we found our way home easily. Like all spirits, the Pixies behave according to their own rules and should not be expected to conform to human logic or morals.

There are also the discarnate spirits who have lived as humans and spirits of our ancestors and the various classes of spirits described in the grimoires and invoked for magical purposes by magicians.

Working with spirits lies at the heart of traditional witchcraft, although it does not always have a place in some of the modern Pagan witchcraft traditions. It is the ability to contact spirits and work with them, and to walk in the spirit world, that has been the true mark of the witch down the millennia and it is something we share with practitioners of traditional religions in Australia, Africa and the Americas.

When working magic outdoors, I am always aware that the place I have chosen to work in has its own spirits. Every tree, rock and stream has its own guardian spirits. Before I begin working, I will take some time to sense the spirits of the place, honour them and ask their permission to work there. I have chosen my regular working places (or they have chosen me) because of the spirits who live there and I have got to know them. If the spirits of a place do not wish me to work there, I will respect them and move on. Some places have spirits which are known to dislike people intruding on their territory. Most of these places in Devon and the West are known to witches and we respectfully avoid them. Spirits will let you know if they do not want you; you will feel uncomfortable and even physically sick. Perhaps you will lose things or fall over. One such place is Rough Tor on Bodmin Moor in Cornwall. Some years ago a magician from London came down to Cornwall and let it be known that he would be conducting an overnight ritual on Rough Tor. Local witches tried to dissuade him but he would have none of it. He went up the Tor with his tent and magical gear but beat a hasty retreat after a couple of hours when the spirits of the place made it very clear by frightening him half out of his wits that he was not welcome there.

Working with spirits, deliberately contacting them and summoning them up for your magical purposes is a serious business and should not be undertaken lightly. Most true witches work with spirits because it comes naturally to them; they sense and see spirits where others do not and it is as if the spirits have chosen them.

Familiar spirits are those with which the witch has a very close working bond. They are creatures of the spirit world and quite different from living animal familiars. It is quite usual for a witch to have a pet or other animal which works magic with them. Familiar spirits are discarnate beings. The witch will get to know a familiar spirit and form a relationship with it and care for it. In return, the spirit will assist the witch in their magical work. The familiar spirit may inhabit the witch's home. Alternatively, the witch may be able to summon their familiar spirit wherever they are. I learnt from Cecil Williamson how to summon a familiar spirit and work with it. There is no one set rite for this. It is done with very deep magical concentration. The witch first thinks carefully about what kind of spirit s/he wishes to work with. This is very important; what you ask for will surely come to you, so you need to be very clear about this. Then a circle is cast and the spirit is requested to manifest. A working tool or other object may be used to form a link with a familiar spirit. I have a small, unassuming stone which I carry everywhere with me. It is my link with a beloved familiar spirit who has worked with me for many years. If a spirit manifests in an object it may attract your attention by unexpectedly moving the object about; do not be surprised if this happens. You may wish to make a home in your house for a spirit; I will explain how to do this in the chapter on Hearth and Home.

Once you have acquired a familiar spirit and started to work with it, it will tell you its name and you will tell it yours. The spirit's name should never be disclosed to anyone else, not even another witch. The exchange of magical names is a powerful part of spirit working. The witch will have their own magical name. Witches who follow the Wiccan or other coven traditions will have a coven name. This is the name by which they are known in the coven; they take this name at their initiation and it is used by coven members but not disclosed to outsiders. Traditional witches also have their own personal witch name which is known only to themselves and their familiar spirits and not told to anyone else. Choose your witch name carefully because it will be an important part of you: you will grow to be like your witch name. There are many simple traditional witch names which can be found in witch lore and folk and fairy tales. For me, these are preferable to naming yourself after a deity, a pharaoh or a mighty personage from magical history.

Working with spirits should not be done fearfully, because the spirits will sense fear and punish it. It should, however, be done very carefully. Everything you do should be thought through and you should keep your wits about you at all times. Spirits should never be exploited or forced to do things against their will; they will always get their revenge if treated badly.

The witch may acquire an object which already has a spirit living in it. I once bought an old knife with a deer horn handle at an antique fair. I bought it because when I picked it up, the spirit in it immediately spoke to me and would not let me put the knife down. It had a strong feeling of unhappiness about it but it would not let me go. I took the knife home and put it carefully on a table. In the middle of the night I was awakened by a crash. The knife was on the floor on the other side of the room. Nothing else had been disturbed; the doors and windows were closed and no physical being could have entered the room. I tried to soothe the knife and went back to bed. The same thing happened twice more. I eventually took the knife upstairs with me and slept, somewhat nervously, with it by my bed. Cecil Williamson's advice was straightforward. He said the spirit in the knife was unhappy, but that it had clearly chosen me and that I should slowly get to know it and find out what the trouble was. The next night I told the knife my witch name before I went to bed, and, on Cecil's advice, slept with it under my pillow. I awoke two hours later to hear a voice speaking the spirit of the knife's name. I thanked it and went back to sleep. On successive nights the knife told me in dreams about its history. It had had several owners and the last one had been very unpleasant. Over some weeks, the knife and I formed a close bond and it and I have worked together ever since. It had been listened to and its difficult past had been acknowledged and it rewarded me with deep and powerful magic. An object inhabited by a spirit, or which links the witch to a spirit should be looked after carefully. It should be kept away from prying eyes, never used to impress people and always kept clean and free from damage. I usually make fabric or leather containers for such objects; this is part of honouring the spirits.

As well as working with spirits which manifest in our world, there may be times when the witch leaves this world and enters the spirit world. The spirit world co-exists with ours but is very different. Some places are gateways between this world and that of the spirits. These places may be well-known: the fairy raths or hills of Ireland and Scotland, for example, and certain Tors on Dartmoor or standing stones. These places should be approached carefully; folklore is full of advice about this. The old tales contain many stories of people who went to fairy hills on midsummer's eve, or at midnight on a full moon and found themselves in the spirit world. Other gateways to the spirit world may come into existence in unexpected places at a particular time and the witch may pass through them without realising (but will realise very rapidly once the threshold has been crossed that they have left this world).

I have never deliberately chosen to enter the spirit world, but I have on several occasions entered it unawares. Once in a forest I know well I wandered around in the early morning looking for a place to work and found myself in a part of the forest where I had never been before. Colours, sounds and smells seemed subtly different. A path led between two arching oak trees which I had not seen before. It glowed with a thin, greyish light. I followed it to a clearing. It was autumn in the everyday world, but here the trees were in new leaf and the grass seemed much greener than it should have been. I realised I had entered the spirit world. There were lights in the trees in the distance which seemed to be calling me on; I could hear voices whispering and I had a strong urge to go deeper into this wood. Then I was overwhelmed with a sense of how dangerous this very attractive place was. I turned round and went back until I reached places I knew. It was going dark. I had been there all day but it felt as if only a few minutes had passed. I went back the next day, but could not find the two oak trees again.

Be very careful about entering the spirit world. It is a dangerous place, especially for clever witches who think they can cope with anything. One of the dangers is that you may not be able to leave. Time works very differently there and a few minutes in the spirit world may equate to a very long time in the everyday world. I would counsel against entering the spirit world deliberately. If you find yourself there unawares as I did, be very careful and leave after a short time. Do not be afraid but keep all your wits about you. Witch lore and the fairy tales give good advice which should always be followed. Beware of being led deeper and deeper into the spirit world. Never eat or drink anything there as this will prevent you from leaving. Do not enter into bargains or promise anything to beings you meet there. The spirit world works by its own rules which humans find very difficult to understand, and it will impose its lessons harshly and without pity. However knowledgeable or experienced a witch may be, being drawn into the spirit world will be an immense test and it should be treated with the utmost respect.

Working Places

Witches work in two kinds of place: their homes (of which more later) and in outdoor places. Outdoor working places should be chosen carefully. They can be anywhere and it is important to find places close to where you live where the Gods and spirits can be honoured. I have worked in many places in Devon: fields, hilltops, forests, moorland and beaches. The first, essential step is to find a place where the spirits will welcome you and want you to work and you should be able to sense this easily. Like most witches, I work mainly at night, so I like to choose places where sunset and moonrise can be seen easily. One working place is close by an ancient wood on Dartmoor. It is level grassland, over a mile from the nearest road and bounded by a stream in the west and the wood in the north. Beyond the wood are two high, breast-shaped granite tors. Another working place on the southern edge of Dartmoor is a small oak and ash wood situated between a small lake in the east and a river in the west which flows steeply over rocks from north to south. The sea can be glimpsed in the distance in the south. Once when working there, my coven was observed by two inquisitive badgers who stood and watched the whole rite without moving. Another place is a circular clearing in a forest surrounded by huge oak and ash trees. Another is a hilltop in east Devon with rowan and thorn trees. Another is a quiet pebble beach where the full moon rises over the sea, making a silver bridge across the water. All of these places are, as tradition states, bounded by running water. All of them except the beach are watched over by thorn and elder trees. A place which is worked in regularly will become cherished and will welcome you.

Working places may be chosen for specific occasions or purposes. At the dark of the moon I go to an isolated three way crossroads and leave offerings to the Goddess Hecate. The worship of Hecate as a witch Goddess originated with the ancient Greeks. The Romans called her Hecate Trivia (which means Hecate of the Three Ways) and she was honoured where three roads met. My Hecate's crossroad is a deserted, unassuming place where three old, narrow Devon lanes with high hedges meet, and I honour the Goddes and leave honey cakes and wine for her as people have done since the earliest times. My coven once worked a Lammas rite on a small beach just across the Tamar estuary from Plymouth. The Tamar is the great river which divides Devon and Cornwall. It rises near the North Cornish coast and flows southwards; all of the waters of the western side of Dartmoor flow into it. It is a mighty power and is honoured as the goddess Tamara. We travelled there by ferry and worked a harvest rite at high tide as the full moon rose over the estuary. Offerings of barley, wheat and roses were plaited together and given to the water where the sea and the great river met as the high spring tide reached its peak.

The Tolmen (which means "holed stone" in the old Cornish/British language) is a traditional initiation place on Dartmoor. It is a huge glacial boulder wedged into the bank of the Teign river near its source. In its centre is a vertical hole, big enough for a person to clamber through. Witches seeking initiation with us have to climb through the hole as tradition dictates three times. This involves edging one's way carefully along a narrow ledge inches above the fast flowing river then hauling oneself up through the hole. This place has always been used by witches and has its own strong magic which anyone of a magical disposition can immediately sense.

I tend not to work as (many modern Pagans do) in ancient stone circles. I like to leave those to their original makers and their spirits. I might practise sitting out at these places, but I do not like to impose my own rituals on them. The one exception to this for me is the Rollright Stones in Oxfordshire, which have been loved and tended by witches for centuries and where witches still gather. I prefer to find my own, wild places. Cecil Williamson taught me how to find what he called "pulse spots". These are places where the Earth's heartbeat can be sensed very strongly. Pulse spots cannot be found on maps (like ley lines are) but have to be sought out by the witch. To find a pulse spot the witch takes their wand or staff and places the bottom of it on the ground and the top on their forehead. If the place is a pulse spot they will be able to feel the pulse of the Earth through the staff or wand. This should be done quietly and not rushed. With a little practice it becomes easy. All of my regular working places are pulse spots. The heartbeat of the earth will be stronger in some places at certain times of the year and I have learnt over the years to recognise this quality in particular places. At one spot in the forest, the heartbeat is quite markedly at its strongest in the days leading up to Halloween, so I will work there at that time.

There are also some places where I will go to seek the advice of the spirits. These are quiet, out of the way places which most people would not give a second glance to; perhaps an unassuming corner of a field, or a moorland boulder next to a thorn tree, or a particular spot on the bank of a stream, but they are places where I have met with spirits before and know that if I go respectfully I will receive wise counsel and help with my magic.

Working places should be treated with great respect. I like to leave as few traces of my working behind me as possible. If a fire is lit, turf will be removed gently and replaced afterwards, or a fire basket or portable barbecue which can be taken home afterwards will be used. If I use candles (which I rarely do outdoors) they are kept in containers so that wax is not left behind. Candle wax dripped onto trees or old stones is difficult to remove. It will damage wood and stone and will kill lichen which has taken many years to grow. Offerings of food and drink are left for the spirits but they are always things such as grain and wine or water which will sink into the earth or decay very quickly. Leaving obvious offerings or traces of ritual and magic seems to me to be a bad idea, partly because witchcraft is always worked in harmony with nature as much as possible, and partly because witchcraft is not done ostentatiously or for others to see (if it is, it tends not to work). "Leave only your footprints" is wise advice.

The elements

There are four physical elements: air, fire, water and earth. They are a fundamental part of magic making. Since the earliest times witches have recognised that we and the world in which we live are made up of these elements. The elements also have more abstract qualities which make up our personalities associated with them. Air is the mind and the rational intellect, fire is passion, action and creativity, water is emotion, love and the spiritual part of us, and earth symbolises all the things that flow from our physical beings: nurturing and fertility and how we work with the earth on which we live. Understanding the elements and working with them is a very important part of any magical working and will repay deep study.

Sometimes witches rather overlook the elements. There can be a sense that they are something basic that witches learn about at the beginning of their training before they move on to bigger things. This is a mistake. Working with the elements should be part of all magic; never underestimate their power and importance. Hereward Wake taught me that if working magic becomes difficult, or the witch becomes tired or jaded, they should return to simple elemental working to refresh their practice. This is very wise advice which has always worked for me. It is also very logical, because the elements are the substances from which we and the world around us are made, so by working with them we are working with our whole beings.

One of the first steps in learning magic is to work with each of the elements in turn, visualising it and experiencing it until the witch understands the elements as thoroughly as possible. Experiencing each element physically as well as studying its spiritual and symbolic aspects is very important. This can begin with very basic actions: breathing in fresh air deeply, lighting and tending a fire, drinking cold, clear water from a spring, letting earth run through the fingers. The witch can move on and learn more specialist skills associated with the elements. One member of my coven found that she had an aversion to the element of fire, so she concentrated for a while on working with it. After several weeks of intensive work she very proudly participated in a fire walk and came to love and value fire as much as the other elements. I return to elemental working regularly and find it a very enriching part of my work. Just as celebrating the solar year works great changes in the witch, so working with the elements will do too.

Each element has one of the cardinal compass directions associated with it. In most western forms of witchcraft air is associated with the east, fire with the south, water with the west and earth with the north. This may, however vary in some traditions. The important thing is to do what feels right and natural to you. Each element also has a colour attributed to it. The usual western attributions are yellow for air, red for fire, blue for water and green for earth, but this will again depend on tradition and on what feels appropriate. The fifth element is spirit; your spirit.

The Circle between the worlds

The circle is the space within which the witch works. The witch creates a place outside time and space by casting and hallowing a circle. The circle can be cast anywhere; outdoors, in your home, or wherever and whenever you need to do it. In witchcraft the circle is cast to create a sacred working space, and to honour the gods, the spirits and the elements. It is also a protection; nothing can enter the circle unbidden.

The circle represents the witch's universe. It articulates the great circles of time (lunar, solar, tidal and the great aeons) and space, and the witch stands at its centre. There are many different rites and forms of words for casting the circle; all of them contain the same essential processes. It is usual to cast the circle in a sunwise or deosil (clockwise) direction, but if lunar rites are being worked the circle may be cast anti-clockwise, mirroring the apparent motion of the moon around the earth. It is a common misconception that an anticlockwise or widdershins circle is only used for magic of negative intent, or to summon demonic forces. As with many aspects of witchcraft, the direction in which the circle is cast is down to both personal choice and the tradition one follows. The circle may be cast silently with all words spoken inwardly in the mind; when working alone and in a wild place this can be the most effective way to do it. Alternatively, spoken words can be used, and this is the usual practice in group working. Many covens have powerful and beautiful circle casting rituals handed down from generation to generation. Whether the circle is cast silently, or with full ritual words, it is the magical will that really does the work. If words are used, they should be memorised. Scrabbling around with a piece of paper desperately trying to recall the right formula destroys the concentration and detracts from true magical working.

Different traditions of witchcraft may specify the size of the circle. Some traditions specify that the circle should be nine feet (three yards) in diameter and this can easily be marked out with string and a stick. It is sometimes suggested that the nine foot circle was introduced into witchcraft when Gerald Gardner established Wicca, but this size of circle is specified in some of the medieval grimoires so it clearly has a longer magical history. I take a practical approach and fit the circle to the place I am working in. If I am working outdoors the circle will encompass the whole space I wish to use. If I am sitting in front of my fireplace the circle will be not much larger than my body space. I do not usually physically draw a circle when working outdoors as when I am working in the forest or on the moors I do not wish to disturb the ground. I make an exception when working on the beach and draw a circle in the sand as I like the idea that it will be taken by the tide after I have finished. It is essential before casting the circle to know where north is. It should be easy to work this out from the position of the sun, moon and stars, but if none of these are visible, a compass can be used. I then mark each of the four cardinal directions in some way. On my favourite pebble beach in East Devon I make small cairns of stones. In the forest or on the moors I mark north with my staff and then places stones or other found objects at the other quarters. These will be put back in their original places when I have finished so that no traces of my working are left behind. Circle casting is a personal matter and you should do what feels right to you. My main concern is to work in harmony with the place and its spirits, and not impose myself or my preordained ideas on it. If approached in a respectful manner, the working place will always provide what is needed. If I am working indoors I will place an altar in the north and mark each of the cardinal directions with candles of the appropriate elemental colour.

The first step in circle casting is to rid oneself and the working place of all extraneous, distracting and negative thoughts and energies. If working in a group, all the members should be at peace with one another; magic cannot be worked effectively if there is animosity present. The space is cleansed. This is often done by sweeping with a broomstick around the circle. It can also be done simply by pacing around the circle with a purposeful stamping tread. This can be accompanied by a chant.

If working indoors, candles are then lit at each of the elemental quarters. I dispense with candles when working outdoors. In my experience, however protected candles are, they still tend to go out and constantly re-lighting them destroys concentration.

Next, salt and water are consecrated. The water is consecrated first and then the salt. Then the salt is poured into the water and sprinkled around the perimeter of the circle. All those present are then consecrated with the salt and water. This may be done simply by marking the forehead of each person present, or ritual wording and marks specific to the tradition may be used.

Then each of the four elements is taken around the circle and presented to each of the four directions. Incense may be used for air, a candle or burning brand for fire, water is presented in a chalice or other container, and for earth a stone or some earth is used.

Next the witch casts the circle. This is done with great concentration of the magical will. The witch may do this using a staff, wand or athame (ritual knife). If one of these tools is used, it will be one which is very personal to the witch, never used by anyone else, and which contains their personal witch power. The circle can also be cast without tools, simply using the hand. To cast my circle I move slowly, deliberately with my arm outstretched and with my magical will focused and concentrated. I begin between north and east. As I go round the circle, I visualise a line of light flowing from my hand or wand. This builds up as I walk around the circle and flows upwards and around me until when the circle is completed I am within a sphere of light. Sometimes, depending on the purpose of the working, I may visualise light of a particular colour. For a working at the dark of the moon I may visualise darkness rather than light. There are many forms of ritual words used for this part of the circle casting in group working. The one which I was taught, and which is used by many covens is:

"I conjure thee o circle of power that thou be a meeting place of love, joy and truth, a rampart between the world of men and the realms of the mighty ones, a protection that shall preserve and contain the power that we shall raise within thee, wherefore do I bless and consecrate thee in the names of the Old Ones* and the spirits of this place."

* Goddess and God names may be used here.

The quarters and elements are then invoked, beginning in the east. The witch stands in the east, again using a ritual tool or the hand and invokes and honours the spirits of the east/ air.

This process is then repeated in the south, west and north. A form of words which may be used is:

"O ye mighty ones of the east (south, west, north), guardians of air (fire, water, earth), I do summon, stir and call ye up to guard the circle and witness the rite, and I do bid ye hail and welcome."

At each quarter the colour attributed to the element may be visualised, as may the element itself, its spirit or something that symbolises it.

This completes the casting of the circle. When the working is finished, the circle is opened once more, the power that has been raised is returned to earth, and the place becomes part of the everyday world and normal time and space once more. It is important always to remember to do this; it is an essential part of honouring and thanking the gods, the place and its spirits. Gods and spirits are thanked and bid farewell. Then the witch moves round the circle, visualising the light which was summoned up at the circle casting dissipating and returning to earth. At each of the quarters the elemental spirits are thanked and bid hail and farewell. In some traditions this process is done in the same direction as the circle casting; in others it is done in the reverse direction. Any water remaining from the working is offered as a libation. If food and drink have been used in the working, the remains of these are also offered to the working place. After a few moments of quiet contemplation the working is over. The witch may "earth" themselves by eating or drinking something to ensure that they are properly returned from the spirit world. I always return found objects to their original place and leave as few traces of my workings as I possibly can. What I have described here is a full circle casting. If I am working alone outdoors I may simplify the process and work with as few objects and tools as possible, but all the essential steps will take place.

Sitting out

Sitting out, which is also sometimes known as hedge sitting, is a very old magical practice which was practiced by our Anglo Saxon forebears and is at the heart of the older forms of witchcraft. It is a quiet, deceptively simple activity and an art which you should learn to master if you truly want to work with the spirits. Sitting out means finding a quiet, isolated place, sitting there for a long time (several hours or even a whole day) and using the magical mind to commune with the spirits. Witches sit out to work magic, enter the spirit world and seek advice and knowledge.

I have three places which I use for sitting out. One is a hillside in East Devon. A line of ancient oak, beech and ash trees, probably the remains of a very old hedge, grow close together up the hillside and there is a commanding view across a wide valley to the Blackdown Hills. Another place is at the foot of an oak tree in the middle of a large forest. The third is a quiet pebble beach. All of these places have a quality of stillness about them and all of them are pulse spots. They are places where I will not be disturbed by human activity and where I can spend as much time as I want with the spirits.

Like most truly magical activities, sitting out is a slow and quiet process. First you need to choose your place. The next essential step is to still your mind and empty it of everyday, extraneous thoughts. Let the place and the spirits lead you to the right spot. Do not use your conscious mind; let yourself be guided and do not force the process. You will probably choose a pulse spot quite naturally but you may wish to use your staff or wand to feel the pulse. If a place feels unpleasant or difficult to you, move on. The place should be somewhere where you can sit comfortably for a long time. Sitting out means leaving human time and the everyday world behind, so leave phones and watches at home or, if you must have them with you, put them where you cannot see or hear them. Once you have found the place, sit yourself down. Begin by honouring the elements and the four directions, quietly and simply and without speaking. Be as quiet and still as you can, Feel yourself into the place. Observe it as thoroughly as you can. Look around you slowly and notice everything you can see. Do this slowly until all the features of the place are imprinted on your mind and become part of you. Look slowly and carefully at the earth and rocks, the plants and trees, the sky, the view and anything else you can see. Then slowly take in everything you can hear. As you do this you will become aware of small sounds that you did not notice when you first arrived. Then do the same with everything you can smell and feel. Use all of your senses to explore the place. Take as much time as you need to do this. You should not be thinking about time passing, or putting restrictions on the amount of time you have because sitting out will take as long as it takes.

Even if you have visited the place before, this process of using your senses to explore the place is essential. Once this process of observing and sensing the place is completed to your satisfaction you can move on to the next stage. Now you need to relax and completely still your mind. I do this by breathing slowly and deeply. I do not close my eyes but focus on tiny details of the place: a leaf or a blade of grass perhaps, until my conscious mind is no more and I am just part of the place itself.

After a while I will become aware that the place has changed. It is the same place but it has somehow deepened and the spirit aspects of it have become more prominent. Colours, sounds and smells are subtly different. On occasions in this state I have seen the spirits of the place; more often I find that I am able to converse with them. I can ask questions of them and receive answers. At other times it is the place itself, rather than any one spirit which works with me. I may choose to sit out for a particular purpose. Perhaps I have some

34

magical work that I need to do for someone, or an important question that needs an answer. At other times I may decide to sit out with no specific purpose in mind. I sit out for as long as I need to. I usually find that I know quite naturally when it is time to stop, although I will have no idea of how much time has passed. When it is time to stop I gently ease myself back into my normal consciousness. I thank the place and any spirits I have encountered. Before I go, I leave a small offering. This will usually be a small piece of bread, or some flour or rice grains, and a little salt and water. Once I have returned to the everyday world I eat and drink something to "earth" myself and go home to rest as I usually feel very tired after sitting out.

Sitting out is an apparently gently process but, as with all work with the spirit world, it takes practice. You should master the basic magical practices such as circle casting and working with the elements, and be confident of your own abilities before you try it. It is also important to be aware that it is possible to journey very deep into the spirit world through this practice and also that not all spirits will have benign intentions towards you. Even though you will be in what is effectively a light trance state, keep your wits about you. If you encounter anything that you do not like, tell it to be gone and return to the everyday world. Follow the old adage and never eat or drink anything offered to you in the spirit world and do not make foolish bargains or promises.

The Witch's Tools

The only absolutely essential working tool is the magical will and it is possible to work without anything else. However, witches usually have treasured working tools which are used to focus and help the will. I was taught that working tools should always be made. When I first worked as a witch, this was the only option as working tools were not commercially available. These days, a huge variety of working tools, many of them made with great love and care by skilled craftspeople can be bought. I would still recommend making your own working tools. Something you have made yourself will have a power and a truth to it that a tool which has been bought can never have. Even if you do not have craft skills, making your own tools will be very rewarding and I urge you to try it. Hereward Wake made all his own working tools and they had an extraordinary power. The making of magical tools is in itself a magical act. Focus your magical will on every stage of the process and do everything with deliberate magical intent. You may also find items at car boot sales or in junk shops which can be recycled for magical use. Any pre-owned items should be ritually cleansed and then consecrated before you work with them. I always hold an item and try to sense how it has been used before buying it. If it has a negative feeling to it I will not buy it. I usually find that an item which wants to be bought and used will let me know straight away when I pick it up. Tradition states that a witch should never haggle over the price of such an item, but pay what the seller asks. All my magical tools have names which are never spoken to anyone else or written down.

What are the essential witch's tools? In the old traditional forms of witchcraft the two most personal tools which each witch would make for themselves were the staff and the wand. Most people can manage to make both of these things. This means cutting wood and then seasoning and finishing it. When cutting wood, do not be greedy and take only what you need. Always ask permission of the tree spirit before you cut wood. It is traditional to thank the tree for the gift of wood and to leave an offering.

The staff is the primary traditional witch's tool. It is indwelt by a spirit and imbued with its owner's personality. In some traditions it is called a stang. As far as I can ascertain, this is a word from the east and north of England and I have not heard it used in Devon so I refer to mine as a staff. It is made from wood cut from a living tree. It should be of shoulder height and you should be able to hold it comfortably with your arm outstretched. The choice of wood is up to you. Choose wood from a tree with which you have a close affinity. All trees have magical meanings and attributions. You may wish to study the Celtic Tree Alphabet to find out more about this, or your tradition may suggest what you should use. Ash, hazel and oak are often used. All of them are great magical trees. Ash is attributed to the element of air. The Druids used ash staffs. Yggdrasil, the great World tree of Norse mythology was an ash and our Norse and Saxon forebears used it to make rune staves for divination. Hazel is attributed to water and is associated with wisdom. Oak is attributed to earth or air and is the great protective tree from which doors are made. It is closely associated with lightning. It is also the tree of Dionysus, Lord of the vine and intoxication. Wine and beer barrels are made from oak.

Choose a wood which feels right to you but also be practical and choose a wood which is strong and which will dry well.

My staff is made of ash, which is the most common tree in the forests around my home and with which I have a close affinity. Ash is a very strong, vigorous tree, full of power and energy. In the dense, old Devon forests honeysuckle grows in spirals around the ash branches. The ash in its turn grows in spirals around the honeysuckle, forming beautifully twisted spiral curves.

My staff is a thick ash branch with nine spirals. It was cut on Mayday and the honeysuckle which was twisted around and into it carefully removed. I then peeled the bark from the staff and left it to season in a dark dry place. "Season" means just that, Leave the wood for at least a season until it is dry and hard. Do not be tempted to rush this process or the wood will split. When the wood was ready I sanded it smooth and finished it with beeswax and polished it. All these processes were done by hand as I prefer this to using power tools. Working by hand takes longer, but thoroughly imbues the staff with its owner's personality and magical energy. The staff can be stained or varnished if you wish but I prefer natural beeswax. Before use the staff should be shod with iron. This means hammering an iron nail into its base. When I cut my staff, I asked a spirit of the ash to come with it. The last stage of the process is to consecrate the staff and welcome and honour its indwelling spirit. I did this in the forest, under the tree from which the staff had been cut. The staff has many uses. It can be stood in the ground to make an altar when working outdoors, or used for circle casting, or to summon the spirits. A good staff will teach its owner how it should be used. A staff will often have a forked tip, or a forked piece of deer antler can be fixed to the top. A holed witchstone or beads can also be attached to the top of the staff with leather thonging.

The wand is also a powerful personal tool which is cut from a living tree in the same way as the staff. It is associated with the element of fire in some traditions and with air in others. It should measure the same length as from the tip of its owner's middle finger to their elbow. The choice of wood is up to you. In Addition to ash, hazel and oak, rowan, holly and blackthorn are all often used. I have two wands, one of hazel and one of blackthorn. I use the blackthorn specifically for banishing. The tip of the wand may be carved if you wish. An acorn could be carved at the tip of an oak wand, for example. Hands and phalli may also be carved. A stone or a piece of deer antler may be set into the tip of the wand. My blackthorn wand was cut from the cliffs on the Lizard in Cornwall and I set a piece of serpentine from the beach at nearby Kynance Cove into its tip. A very traditional phallic wand is made by fixing a pine cone to the tip of the wand. This is a fiddly process which involves very carefully drilling into the base of a pine cone (not at all easy), fixing a screw into it, and then screwing the other end of the screw into the tip of the wand. Hereward Wake was adept at this, and I still have his pine cone wand which is used by my coven. The more the wand can be associated with the personality of its owner and the places where they work, the better. I prefer not to use commercially bought crystals for wand tips as I do not know under what circumstances they have been mined, and they have no local associations for me, but this is a matter of personal choice. The wand, like the staff, has many magical uses including circle casting, invoking gods and spirits, finding pulse spots and consecrating spells and charms, As with the staff, the wand will guide its owner in its use.

In the modern Wiccan traditions the athame or black handled knife is the primary personal working tool and is used instead of the wand. Like the wand, it is associated with air or fire. Making or obtaining an athame is an important task undertaken before the first Wiccan initiation. I have to admit that forging a blade is a skill which is way beyond me, so when acquiring an athame I did not stick with my usual rule of making everything. My first athame was a simple French fruit peeling knife. I was staying in a small town in Brittany and dreamed that I bought my athame from a market stall. I awoke to find a market taking place in the street below and sure enough, there was a stall selling knives. I sanded down the wooden handle, painted it black and etched into it the signs traditionally used on the athame handle in Wicca. This tool served me well for a number of years. It was eventually replaced by an iron blade forged by a Wiccan smith which I set into a black deerhorn handle which I made myself. If you can learn to forge your own blade, then you can make the whole thing yourself. The athame is used for the same purposes as the wand. It should be kept carefully wrapped in a cloth and away from prying eyes. The athame is never used by anyone other than its owner. When a witch dies, their wands or athames are traditionally broken so that no one else can use them and either buried with the witch or returned to one of their special places or cast into the sea or running water.

The cup or chalice represents the element of water and is used to hold wine, mead or other liquid which is consecrated and drunk during rituals. A chalice can be made using clay if you have pottery skills or turned and carved from wood. A traditional Devon form of chalice is an old horn cup. These were in common use in rural areas from medieval times onwards and were often used for medicines. They can still be bought cheaply in junk shops and at antique fairs. The Museum of Witchcraft in Boscastle has a fine collection of them.

The pentacle is a platter or disc which represents the element of earth. It is used in rituals to hold food and objects or spells can be placed on it for charging and consecration. The pentacle should be made from wood, clay or metal and has a series of symbols carved, painted or burnt into it.

A very effective pentacle can be made from a wooden breadboard with the symbols burnt into it using a pyrography tool, or simply painted onto it. My pentacle is made of a large slice of wood, about half an inch thick, taken from the trunk of a fallen oak tree which had come down in a storm and which a neighbour of mine was cutting up for logs.

Another item which I consider to be essential is a notebook or journal. Most witches have a book in which they write down all the rituals and magical lore handed down to them plus their own rites and workings. In Wicca this book is called the Book of Shadows and one of the new witch's first tasks after their initiation into a coven is to copy out by hand their initiator's Book of Shadows.

This is a very effective practice; copying by hand helps the witch to become really familiar with the material and think about it in depth. It is a pity that some contemporary covens dispense with this practice and instead give the new witch an electronic copy of the book or printed papers. This is no substitute for hand copying; the old ways are certainly best in this instance. A notebook or journal is also essential when learning witchcraft. In it, you can record details of your magical work and any dreams or important experiences you have.

Throughout this book you will see that I refer to making notes in your journal. You will look back on these over the months and years and learn an immense amount from them. I have journals going back over nearly thirty years of magical practice and I read them frequently and always learn from them. Your journal and/ or your Book of Shadows should be personal to you and not shown to anyone except other witches. There is no need to spend a lot of money on expensive notebooks and as with all working tools, the more personal they are to you, the better. You can buy a hardback notebook or sketchbook and make a cover for it using cloth or a collage of your favourite images. You can also make a notebook yourself. To do this, cut sheets of paper to double the page size that you want. Make a similarly sized cover from card and decorate it. Fold the pages and cover down their centres. Then, using a large needle and strong thread, sew the book together down the centre fold.

There are various other useful items which you may wish to acquire or make. A cauldron is a very traditional witch's possession. In the days when boiling water, brewing and cooking were done over an open fire, the cauldron would be used for many practical purposes. If you have an open fire and a large fireplace, you can hang a cauldron over the fire and use it to brew herbal spells. If you want to use a cauldron outdoors, you will need to make a metal tripod to hang it over your fire. The cauldron can also be used without fire to hold spells. It is not a good idea to light a fire inside a cauldron (as I have seen some witches do) as they are not designed for this and may be damaged. Old cauldrons can be bought in antique and junk shops, but can be expensive. I have yet to meet a witch who has made their own cauldron; if you are out there, I salute you.

Another item I find useful is a magnifying glass. I use mine to catch fire from the sun and to burn spells which need the power of the sun onto paper or wood. I found an old magnifying glass at a car boot sale and decorated the handle with a pyrography tool.

A stock of jars and bottles for spells and herbs is useful. Old jars and bottles can be found at car boot sales and junk shops. Old medicine bottles, especially blue and green ones, work well. Jam jars are also good. Jars and bottles should have good, airtight stoppers or lids and should be thoroughly washed and dried before use.

Many of my spells involve tying knots, sewing, knitting and plaiting so I keep a stock of yarn, embroidery thread and fabric for these purposes. I also have a couple of needles which are reserved for magical work.

I have two other personal tools which I use a lot. One is a mirror which is used for looking, reflecting the moon and the sun and scrying and spell making. The use of mirrors is explained in more detail in later chapters of this book. My mirror is a basic handbag mirror, probably dating from the 1960s, in a plastic scallop shell shaped holder, which I bought for pennies in a junk shop. This might seem rather kitsch to some people, but I knew it was right for me as soon as I found it. Years ago I was helping a friend round up some sheep on a farm in the Blackdown Hills in East Devon. At the top of the pasture on the ridge of the Blackdowns stood a line of ancient oak trees. As I walked along by the trees my foot caught in something and I tripped and fell full length. I pulled at the thing that had tripped me. It was a smooth and shiny piece of oak tree root shaped like a hand with five fingers. As soon as I held it I felt an immense connection with it. It had attracted my attention in no uncertain manner. It became one of my most treasured magical tools. I use it to cast spells. Sometimes I place spells or other objects on it for charging. At other times I rub the hand whilst repeating the spell I wish to cast.

Candles, herbs and incenses are also important in working magic. You can make candles yourself if you wish. You can source the equipment and materials from any good craft shop.

Simple candles can be made by rolling sheets of honeycomb beeswax, which can be obtained from beekeepers or craft suppliers, around length of candle wick. The beeswax should be very gently softened, but not melted. For more advanced candle making you will need moulds, wax, dyes and a double boiler pan. Scented candles can be made by adding a few drops of essential oils to the mix.

I collect and dry herbs I wish to use and keep stocks of ones that I use frequently and have an affinity with. I grow some of them in my garden; others are gathered from the wild. I use them medicinally, and in spells, charms and incenses. Every herb, bark and plant resin is part of the system of magical correspondences and has its own attributions to elements, days, times, planets and deities. There are many good herbals available from which you can learn about the magical and medicinal properties of herbs, or this knowledge may be handed down to you as part of your tradition. As with all organic materials, when gathering herbs take only what you need and thank the plant. Every living herb has its own spirit and you should respectfully ask its permission before you cut it. Cut herbs carefully and do not pull plants up by the roots. Herbs are best gathered in the morning on a warm dry day, although you may also wish to gather them at night or other times for specific magical purposes. Herbs should be tied in bundles and hung upside down in a dark, dry place to dry. When dried, they should be placed in glass jars with airtight lids away from direct sunlight.

Incense is used in most magical work. Making your own is not difficult and incense made with magical intent will increase the power of your work. Loose incense burned on charcoal blocks is always preferable to commercially made joss sticks. Charcoal blocks are available from magical or church suppliers. They should be placed in a heatproof incense burner or other suitable container. A large seashell works well. Hereward Wake used a simple copper bowl filled with sand. Use tongs when lighting them and be careful as they get very hot and can pop and fizz. The charcoal block should be glowing when you place the incense on it; wait until any flames and smoke have died down.

Incenses normally consist of one or more dried herbs, flowers or barks and a gum or resin. Gums and resins used in incense include frankincense, myrrh, gum benzoin or gum arabic. These can also be bought from magical or church suppliers. A few drops of essential oils can also be used if you wish. A simple altar incense can be made from three parts frankincense, two parts dried rose petals, one part lavender and a pinch of gum benzoin. The making of incense is a magical act and every step of this process should be carried out with focused magical intent. Crush the frankincense and gum benzoin to powder with a pestle and mortar. Then add the other ingredients, mix them together and store them in a dry, airtight jar until you are ready to use them. You can experiment with your own incense blends for your own magical purposes. Making incense is a wonderful activity which will have a profound effect on your magical practice. As your knowledge of herbs and other plant materials deepens, you will create special incense blends to honour your gods and work your magic.

The Moon

The moon plays an immense part in our lives and in witchcraft. The moon's gravitational pull causes tides which peak every twelve hours; these affect not only the sea but the earth and our own bodies. The moon's monthly journey around the earth during which we see it first as a new crescent, then as the bright and glorious full moon, and then as the waning old moon also governs some of the more hidden aspects of our lives. The moon has a profound effect on the growth of plants and research has shown that its light governs the menstrual cycles of women. Lunar time is the first time that we know. Before we are born we live in our mother's womb governed by moon time, before we see the light of the sun. Babies are most usually born at exactly the same phase of the lunar cycle at which they were conceived. The oldest calendars, made in palaeolithic times, were records of the lunar cycle carved onto pieces of bone. Before we messed the system up by introducing artificial light at night, it was the light of the full moon which triggered ovulation in women and menstruation would occur at the old/ new moon.

The link between the moon and women is a very profound one. The moon is venerated as a goddess around the world and she is at the heart of many traditions of witchcraft. Over the millennia she has been known by many names: Selene, Isis, Diana, Artemis, Neith, Hera, Aphrodite, Amaterasu, Ceridwen, Io, Ishtar and Juno are just a few of the goddesses who have been associated with the moon. Pre-christian paganism, especially in classical Greece and Rome, venerated the moon as patroness of women, mistress of childbirth, and goddess of the sea and all waters, and she presided over the planting and harvesting of crops. To witches she is all these things but even more. She is held especially to be our goddess and protectress. Witchcraft ceremonies usually take place at night, by the light of the moon, and witches mark the full moon with a monthly Esbat rite. Many mark the new and dark moons too. She is venerated by many as a triple goddess, having three phases (new, full and old) which mirror the phases of the lives of women: maiden, mother and elder. Magic is made at night, either by the light of the moon or in the darkness when she is not visible but her gravitational pull is still felt. Throughout its history, witchcraft has been seen as a lunar tradition and witches celebrate the moon's links with intuition, inspiration and inner vision. The power of witchcraft is in many ways the power of the moon.

Living by the moon

Lunar time is gentle and quiet; less obvious than the bright light of the sun and the round of the solar year, but it is ever present and works its constant changes in all of us. Its link with the menstrual cycle of women is obvious but it also affects men too, the full moon especially.

In order to be aware of lunar time you need to use a lunar calendar. Many diaries and almanacs include lunar phases. It is easy to download a lunar calendar from the internet, but it is also good to make your own as a way of recognising and honouring the part the moon plays in your life. A lunar calendar arranges the year into lunar months, so that the phase of the moon is the most important thing, rather than mapping lunar months onto the solar calendar. You can make a simple lunar calendar by making a list of the new, first quarter, full and last quarter moons for the year so that you have a year of lunar months rather than solar ones. You can take this further by drawing a line of small circles for each lunar month. The easiest way to do this is to use a stencil, which can be bought cheaply from an art supplier. Then shade your circles to show the phases of the moon, and arrange the calendar dates around them. There will usually be between twelve and thirteen lunar months in any solar year so an A4 lunar calendar is reasonably easy to make.

The simple act of making a lunar calendar and being aware of the moon's phases seems like a very small thing, but it will make you much more aware of lunar time and the effect the moon has on you and the world around you. It will gently but profoundly alter your relationship with the moon and the world in which you live and is one of the important bases of experiential witchcraft. Witchcraft means being aware of moon time and the subtle interplay between it and the solar year and the changing seasons. You can help this process along by keeping a moon diary in which you note significant experiences and events (especially those connected to your magical work) and your dreams and relate them to the phase of the moon. I ask all the people I train to do this for up to a year. At first it may seem tedious or its relevance may not be clear, but as months pass it becomes a vital guide to the person's development as a witch and often people will continue it beyond the agreed time period. If you are a woman you can mark your menstrual periods on your lunar calendar too. You may find that as you become more aware of the moon in your life, your periods may come into phase with the moon. Men may find that they have a marked period of energy, creativity and increased sexual drive around the time of the full moon. Once you become aware of these patterns, you can use them in your magical work. Deepening your experience of moon time will also help you overcome the crazy, damaging notion that our minds and bodies are separate things, and that the mind is somehow superior to the body. Understanding that the mind and body are one essential entity will be an important part of your development as a witch.

You can take this process further if you wish. Noting that it was artificial night lighting which had destroyed the link between western women's menstrual cycles and the moon, American writer Louise Lacey pioneered "Lunaception" which she formulated as a "natural" system of contraception. I tried it, somewhat sceptically, in the mid 1970s when my interest in witchcraft was beginning and I wanted to bring myself into phase with the lunar cycle (but not as a method of contraception!). I was amazed to find that it worked. Lacey's method was to sleep in a totally dark room (she advocated blackout curtains) from day one to day thirteen of a lunar cycle, counting the new moon as day one. She then slept with a nightlight on for days fourteen, fifteen and sixteen of the lunar cycle, which are the time of the full moon. Then she reverted to sleeping in total darkness until the last day of the moon. This mimicked the effect of moonlight so that ovulation occurred at the full moon and the menstrual period at the very end of the lunar cycle.

I was living in a city in the English midlands at the time, with plenty of artificial night lighting, but Lacey's system really worked for me and brought my cycle into phase with the moon. Soon after this I moved from the city to a part of the countryside which is very dark at night and found that my cycle maintained the lunar link without any need for blackout curtains if I simply slept in the light of the full moon each month. I have done this ever since and consider it to be an essential part of my magical practice. I also noticed a strong link between my menstrual cycle and my dreams, with strong and important dreams, with a specific range of colours and magical symbols, occurring in the week before my period. I documented this in a work called *Water Into Wine*.

The daily tidal rhythm of the moon can also be used. I lived by the sea when I was a child and realised from a very early age that I could feel the tidal rhythm whether or not I could see the sea. The high tide induced a feeling of brimming, full excitement and energy, which passed as the tide began to ebb, and the low tide created a calm, peaceful feeling. Years later I noticed the same feelings in an office in the centre of Bristol where I worked and organised my work around them. If you live reasonably close to the sea, which most people in Britain do, you can obtain tide tables for the coast nearest to you. This certainly works in Devon where the local television stations include tide times as part of their daily weather forecasts. Remember that the tides affect our bodies and the earth as well as the sea and learn to use the tidal rhythms in your magic. Ebb tides are for banishing and letting things go; let the water wash that which you need to be rid of out with the tide. Rising tides are for attracting things to you and drawing up the power of the incoming tide into a strong magical focus. The high tide and the period of slack water that follows it are ideal moments for ritual. Remember that tides happen wherever you are, not just by the sea.

There is a deeper magical understanding which underlies the daily tidal rhythm. Witches and occultists understand that there are also eternal tides behind life, death and rebirth that operate ceaselessly. We are born, die and reborn again according to the will of our Goddess. The life that we are currently living is just one small phase in the great tide of existence. The tidal rhythms of the sea and the moon remind us of this underlying reality and when we honour the Moon Goddess we think of our part in the greater processes of the universe. This is expressed very clearly in the work of the 20th century occultist Dion Fortune. Her magical novel, *The Sea Priestess*, has at its heart a great ritual to the Moon Goddess as mistress of the tides. Her invocation of this goddess is used in many contemporary witchcraft rituals. Indeed, many witches use Fortune's words without being aware of who wrote them.

My coven celebrated Dion Fortune's "Sea Priestess" rite at Brean Down, where Fortune set the novel; a long promontory on the North Somerset coast which juts out into the Severn Estuary. This is an excellent place to work with the tides, as the Severn has the second highest tidal range in the world. Although Brean Down is close to large towns and cities, it has an extraordinary remoteness and the strength of the tides is ever present. There is also a very real sense of the power and danger of the sea there.

We chose a full moon close to the Spring Equinox and began in mid-morning at low tide. Each person had written out and learnt Fortune's Sea Priestess invocation and we made Fire of Azrael incense according to Fortune's instructions (sandalwood, juniper and cedar) which we placed in a container made of biodegradable modelling clay. We found a secluded place just above the high tide line on the low cliffs at the furthest seaward tip of Brean Down. We placed the Fire of Azrael as close as we could to the sea at low tide. As the tide began to turn we lit the incense and began our rite. We simply repeated Fortune's invocation amongst us and between us ceaselessly as the tide came in. As the tide grew higher we were all drawn together into the deep world of the tides and the moon. We remained there for six hours. Sometimes we were speaking the invocation, and sometimes we were in a tidal, lunar reverie. During the rite the sea took the Fire of Azrael. When the high tide peaked, the rite ended. We thanked the Moon/ Sea Goddess, the spirits of Brean Down, and the spirit of Dion Fortune and left. This was an apparently simple action; there were no elaborate words or procedures, just Fortune's invocation and the incense and ourselves, but it had a profound effect on all of us. We understood that we had opened ourselves up to the power of the moon and the tides, and over the weeks and months which followed it, all of us felt that power in our lives and gained a deep understanding of it and how to live by it. It was marvellous to work this rite in the place in which Fortune had set it, but it could equally be worked in any quiet place close to the sea.

Monthly moon Rites

Witch traditions teach that our rites take place at night because we revere the Moon Goddess above all other powers. It is by the light of the moon, or in the darkness when it is absent, that we understand most fully what it is to be a witch. When the bright, glorious sun has left the sky, then the subtle but pervasive witch powers can be seen and sensed most clearly. Magic done at night, under the moon, may seem quiet and gentle, but its power is immense. Honouring the Moon Goddess, outside at night, whether alone and silently, or in a circle of one's fellow witches, is an essential part of witchcraft. It should never be neglected, and should be a constant part of what you do.

Most contemporary western pagans cast their circles by moving clockwise, or deosil, in the direction of the sun's movement through the sky. When working rites to the Moon Goddess, however, witches may make their circles or dance in an anti-clockwise or widdershins direction, mirroring the moon's visible movement around the earth. There is a misconception that moving widdershins is only associated with demonic magic, or magic with evil intent. Witches who honour the Moon Goddess know different.

Simply standing in the light of the full moon and drinking in its light, or watching the new moon when it is visible as a thin sliver of light after sunset, or gazing at the old moon rising pale and yellow just before dawn, are magical acts in themselves which will bring you into closer communion with the Moon Goddess in all her aspects. Watching the moon rise over the sea, making a pathway of silver light on the water is something I find brings me into a deep understanding of my own relationship with the Moon Goddess and all she signifies. The south-facing coast of East Devon close to my home is a great place to do this, especially at full moon. Try standing looking out over the sea as the full moon rises. As the moon

makes her silver pathway over the waters, experience the full power of her light and her gravitational pull on you. Be present with all your senses. In your mind's eye, travel along the moon path over the sea and up to the moon and commune with her. Don't try to make this complicated or intellectualise it while you are doing it; like most moon magic this is about seeing, feeling, using every sense you have and simply being present in the moment.

The new moon is the time to make new beginnings and the magic worked at this time will be for new departures, to begin new undertakings, and to see and do things afresh. This is the time to clean and refresh altars and working tools and make and dedicate new ones. Seeds are planted, literally and metaphorically, which will grow and develop as the moon waxes. The new moon brings clarity and focus.

The full moon is the time when most witch covens celebrate their monthly Esbat rite, honouring the Moon Goddess in her bright, powerful aspect and as Mother. A ceremony called Drawing Down The Moon is often celebrated, in which the Moon Goddess in drawn down and invoked into one of the female witches of the coven. Magically the full moon is the time of consummation and fulfilment, when things reach their peak and are brought to birth in the world.

The old or dark moon, the time when we can no longer see the moon in the sky, is the time for rest and drawing apart from the world. This is the time when we turn slowly and gently to our dreams and inner visions. Active, dynamic magic is not worked at this time. Rather it is a time for letting go, when we can bid farewell to thoughts, ideas, emotions and things we no longer need and leave them behind. Women whose menstrual cycles are in phase with the moon may also work specific magic connected with menstruation and the old moon.

Living by the moon is an essential part of witchcraft. It will work deep changes and bring real magical rewards.

Lunar planting and harvesting

The link between the moon and the growing of crops is one which has been known since very ancient times and if you are a keen gardener and want to explore this in detail, there are plenty of books and guides available which will tell you how. The very basic principles are that seeds should be sown during the waxing phase of the moon (between new moon and full) and crops harvested in the waning phase of the moon (between full moon and old). The rationale for this is that the waxing moon encourages plants to draw up and retain water and so germination is better and plants grow strong, and that the waning moon makes plants lose water, so that they can be harvested, dried and preserved well. A more detailed, magical version of this system, which is an ancient aspect of Western hermetics and herbalism, incorporates lunar astrology, so that plants which are linked to specific astrological signs are planted and tended when the moon passes through their sign. This is a complex subject, but one which will repay serious study if gardening is part of your magical work. On a general level, harvest any herbs, wood for staffs or wands, and other plant material when the moon is waning, and sow and plant out any crops for magical use when the moon is waxing.

The Moon In The Witch's Mirror

Moon magic can be very simple and direct. Begin by looking at the full moon in a mirror. The witch's mirror is an important magical tool (see the chapter on The Witch's Tools). For moongazing use an ordinary small, silvered mirror, not a dark or black mirror. Any mirror will do. A mirror tile about six inches square is ideal. As with other magical tools it is good to keep the mirror just for this purpose and cover it when it is not in use.

The mirror is used to catch, focus and reflect the light of the moon. Go outside on a bright moonlit night and hold your mirror up to the moon. Find the moon in the mirror and "catch" its reflection. Then still your mind and use the mirror to reflect the light of the moon onto your face and charge yourself with the power of the moon. You can commune directly, without any need for words, with the Goddess of the Moon by this method. This rite is silent, focused and intense. It sounds simple but its effects can be profound, as with much of the best magic.

Using your mirror, you can reflect the light of the moon onto working tools, talismans, charms or other objects which you wish to charge magically with the power of the moon. Again this is best done with silent magical concentration; there is no need for words. You can also use the mirror to reflect moonlight into places it would not normally reach; perhaps onto an altar or shrine or the dark corners of a room. This should be done slowly so that you can really look at what you are doing.

If you work magic with other people, then a group moon mirror rite is a powerful magical experience. Each person in the group will need a mirror. The group stands in a circle in the moonlight. The first person "catches" the moonlight in their mirror and then "passes it on" to the next person in the circle. The moonlight is then passed from person to person until it has travelled all the way around the circle.

Moon mirror rites are best worked at the full moon when the light is brightest, but you can try them at any time when the moon is visible. I recommend that they should be worked in silence, so that the magical will is concentrated as intently as possible on the moon and its light. Always look at the moon in the mirror, rather than directly, as the actions of moving the mirror around and "catching" the moonlight, and the concentrated looking into the small mirror and excluding everything else will heighten the magical effect.

Charging water with the moon

Moon charged water is used in many magical actions, spells and charms. It can be used to consecrate a working place or circle and to bring the power of the moon and the blessings of the Moon Goddess down into tools, talismans, and other objects.

To charge water with the moon you will need a clean blue glass bottle with a stopper or lid. Blue is the traditional colour for this work and it will protect the water once it has been charged. You will also need pure, clean water, preferably from a well or spring. Fill the bottle with water and place it on a windowsill in the light of the full moon for three nights, asking the blessings of the moon and the Moon Goddess on this work. Leave it there all night.

When daylight comes, wrap the bottle in a dark cloth and put it away in a dark cupboard or box away from the daylight. When you are ready to use your moon charged water make sure that you do not expose it to daylight, keeping the bottle wrapped in a cloth if you need to use it during the day.

You may also choose to charge your working tools and other objects simply by leaving them in the light of the moon. Always ask the blessing of the moon before doing this.

Moon Shadows

When the moon is bright it casts shadows. When the moon is really bright these have a delicate colour. On a moonlit night, stand in the moonlight and cast your moon shadow. What colour is it?

Lunar eclipses

An eclipse of the moon occurs at full moon when the earth passes between the moon and the sun and the earth's shadow covers the moon, cutting off sunlight from the moon. Lunar eclipses occur much more frequently than solar ones and you can easily find details of forthcoming ones in almanacs, newspapers, or on the internet. When a lunar eclipse occurs, the moon is still visible but its light is dimmed and it appears a brownish-red in colour, very reminiscent of blood. A lunar eclipse is referred to as a blood moon in witchcraft and it is an especially powerful time to work magic. It is easy to see why people have been afraid of lunar eclipses over the centuries, and also why they have been traditionally associated with witches (see Shakespeare's *Macbeth*, for example) as the moon appears to go dark and turn to blood.

As with the moon and mirrors, or the rite of the tides, you can begin to experience the power of a lunar eclipse simply by watching one as it happens, from the moment the moon first begins to turn red, right through the duration of the eclipse, until the moon becomes bright again. Doing this quietly, for as long as it takes with no distractions; just being there and observing with all your senses, will have a strong effect on you and bring you into ever closer communion with the deeper, hidden aspects of the Moon Goddess. Making a drawing or painting of the moon during an eclipse can also be a good thing to do. You do not need any great artistic skills; the full moon is a simple circle and you just draw/ paint the colours and light that you can see. I have done this exercise with coven groups where everybody has protested that they can't draw, but all of them have ended up surprised and pleased with the results. Your eclipse drawing or painting can be placed on your altar or put into your magical journal.

Magic worked at a lunar eclipse will be about the deep, hidden aspects of the moon. As you build up your work with the moon, your magical senses will guide you as to what it should be used for. Eclipse magic can be difficult to express in words; experiencing this time and working with whatever it reveals to you is the most important thing. You may choose to see the eclipse as the time when the moon is menstruating and use this time for magic connected with your own moon/menstrual cycle. Men may also find this is a time when they can focus on the dark aspects of the Goddess. It is also an excellent time for banishing things. Tools, water or charms can be charged with the power of the eclipse by leaving them out in its red light. Usually these will be specific things which you wish to use for purposes connected with the blood moon.

The Sea and the Seashore

We have already seen how the sea and its tides are ruled by the moon, and how the magic of these things is intimately linked.

I grew up by the sea and have lived close to it for most of my life. In Devon the sea is never far away; even on the wild heights of Dartmoor and Exmoor the sea can be glimpsed in the distance. Devon has two coasts. The northern one runs from the Cornish border and Hartland Point and then past the Taw and Torridge estuaries and along the northern edge of Exmoor to Somerset, bordering first the Irish Sea and then the great Severn estuary. It has high cliffs, against which many ships have foundered, and immense sandy beaches. The southern coast runs from the Tamar estuary at Plymouth, past the estuaries of the Dart, Teign and Exe rivers and along the "Jurassic Coast" to the border with Dorset. I know all of these places, but it is the southern coast of East Devon, with its pebble beaches and soft, red cliffs, where I go most often to work witchcraft. This is a coastline with quiet, isolated beaches accessed by steep cliff paths, rich in wild flowers, herbs and sloe bushes, where the sound of waves breaking on steeply sloping pebble beaches is ever present. The rocks are full of fossils and the constantly eroding cliffs often reveal mineral treasures. Many of these beaches face south and west, and so are perfect for rituals celebrated at sunset during the summer months.

The seashore is an important place to work magic because it is a liminal space where the land meets the sea; an edge between two worlds. It is never still, always changing; always becoming something new. The tides never cease and the wind and the weather will change the shore from day to day. Most witches tend to work in forests or green fields, perhaps because they feel they are somehow more private. Do not overlook the possibilities of working on the seashore. Working magic on a warm summer's evening around a fire of driftwood on a quiet East Devon pebble beach as the sun sets into the sea is a deep and unforgettable experience.

You can begin your sea magic by sitting out quietly on the sea shore and looking at the sea. This is best done alone. Sit for as long as you can. Clear your mind of extraneous everyday thoughts and simply look, listen and feel. Watch the waves breaking and listen to the sound they make. Be there in the moment. After a while, you will find that your senses become heightened and you will shift into a magical meditative state. Keep any thoughts or images that come to you safe in your mind. If you can manage it, sitting for a whole tide (six hours) is a wonderful and very fulfilling experience. Swimming in the sea (observing reasonable safety rules, of course) can also be done with magical intent.

I have evolved some simple rules for working rituals by the sea. I take as little equipment with me as possible as it can be an encumbrance and detract from my concentration. It is usually possible to find everything I need on the beach. I only take my mirror, a compass and some means of lighting a fire. Driftwood can be gathered for a fire, although a small disposable barbecue is also good on a pebble beach. It will ensure that burn marks are not left on the stones and it will light easily in damp weather. Driftwood can be added to the barbecue once it is lit. I adapt my usual practices to the place I am working in. It seems pointless to invoke water in the west if the sea is in the south so I arrange my circle around the actual environment rather than imposing pre-ordained ideas on it. I always let the spirits of the place guide me in what I do. Cairns of pebbles or small sandcastles can be used to mark the quarters and the circle can be traced in the sand. I prefer to use a stick found on the beach instead of a wand or athame as I like to work with things that the place has given me. I always make sure that no damage is done to the beach and return it to the state I found it in. I take any debris away with me. A circle drawn in sand below the tideline can be left for the sea to remove.

The Sea in the Witch's Mirror

Just as powerful magic can be made by looking at the moon in a mirror, so the spirits can be summoned and magical work performed through looking at the sea in a mirror. Unlike much witchcraft, this can be done in broad daylight, when the bright light of the sun can be caught and reflected and the seashore abounds with the spirits of air and light.

Take an ordinary mirror (as with the moon, a mirror tile will work well) on a sunny spring or summer day. Sit facing the land with your back to the sea and hold your mirror or place it in the ground so that it reflects the sea back at you. Do not look directly at the sea; only at its reflection in your mirror. Do this for as long a time as possible; at least an hour. You will find that observing the sea in your mirror is very different from looking at it directly and that you will gradually slip into a heightened state of consciousness in which you become very aware of the relationship between land, sea and sky, and that you are working at the edge between two worlds. It is in this heightened state that you will begin to notice the bright, ephemeral spirits of air and light, usually around the edges of your mirror. If you focus your looking on the sea, you may find that sea spirits appear. This is quiet and gentle but deep magic, which needs to be done slowly and with concentrated intent. Never rush this kind of work; give it time to work its changes in you.

The Bounty of the Sea

The tides bring in all sorts of treasures which can be used in magic-making: stones, seashells, driftwood and much more. Collecting these things on a seaside walk and using them in your magic can be a wonderful thing to do. Please do not be greedy and take only what you need. A large clam, scallop or oyster shell can make a good incense holder or be used to symbolise water when working, and all manner of treasures from the sea can be used for magic or making magical tools.

Stone

The beach at Budleigh Salterton in East Devon is composed of flat oval grey stones. Many of them have red patches and I once found one with a beautiful red, crescent moon-shaped marking. This became a treasured blood-moon charm which I keep on my altar. Find a special stone which will become important in your magic. A phallic flint (Cecil Williamson always referred to these as cock rocks) can be used to symbolise the god on your altar.

Small flat pebbles can also be used to make rune stones which can be used for divination.

To make rune stones you simply need to collect pebbles of a similar size and shape and paint the runic or another magical alphabet or set of symbols of your choice on them.

Bright, white quartz pebbles are also traditionally used as protective charms and kept by the door of the house or in a special place in the garden. Please do not remove large

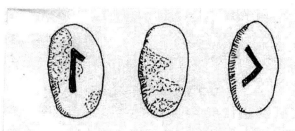

quantities of stones from beaches. Respect the place and its spirits and also remember that one magical stone will be special; lots will dilute your magical intent.

Witch Stones

Throughout Britain, and especially in Devon, stones with naturally occurring holes are traditionally held to be important in magic. In Devon they are usually referred to as witch stones; in other parts of Britain they are known as hag stones or bride stones. The beaches of South and East Devon are rich in witch stones, usually made of flint.

Witch stones are used to protect houses and farm buildings. They were thought to be particularly effective at protecting animals and it is still possible to see witch stones hung up in cow sheds to protect the cows and their milk, or in stables to prevent horse from being ridden at night by the dreaded Night Mare. Most witches will have one somewhere about their house or garden. A witch stone should always be threaded onto a cord, preferably red, to make its magic effective. Threaded witch stones may also be given as good luck charms at weddings or hung up by babies' cots.

When you find a witch stone on the beach, the first thing to do is to thank the spirits for it. Then hold the stone up to your eye and look at the world through it, and see what you can see. Take your witch stone home. Take a strong red thread or cord and pass one end through the hole in the stone. Tie the ends of the thread together, and as you do so, cast a spell for protection. It is tying the ends of the thread together that seals the magic, so be sure to concentrate as you do this. Hang your witch stone somewhere special, perhaps in your hearth or just inside your front door. Witch stones may also be made into necklaces for use in ritual or added to the handles of wands or athames. I like to keep one hanging in my car to keep me safe on the roads. Small witch stones can be threaded onto wire and made into a circle or wreath which can be hung up in the house or garden.

Larger witch stones can also be threaded onto wire to form a witch stone rope. This is a very traditional way of using witch stones and was the usual way of protecting farm buildings and gates.

To make a witch stone rope you will need large witch stones and wire. The number of stones you use is up to you; my own preference is for five, seven or nine, depending on my magical purpose. Cut a piece of wire at least four feet long. Thread the wire through the biggest stone. Place the stone half way along the wire so that the wire forms two strands above it. Now twist the two strands of wire together tightly above the stone repeatedly until the twisted wire is about an inch and a half long. Now thread the next stone onto the wire above the twisted strands. Twist the wire above the second stone.

Repeat these processes until all your stones are threaded. As with all practical magic, you should be concentrating on your magical intent throughout this operation and working with a calm, focused mind. Form a hanging loop with the remaining ends of the wire. Your rope is now ready for use. Holed sea shells can often be found and a similar rope can be made from these and used in sea magic.

Fossils

The East Devon coast is rich in fossils and after winter storms it is often possible to find spiral ammonites, or sea urchins whose markings make a five-pointed star, and other fossil shells and sea creatures at the base of the cliffs. I like to find these when they are naturally washed out of the cliffs or brought in by the tide, but I dislike the now widespread practice of hacking them out of the cliffs with hammers and chisels which seems to me to show little respect for the land.

Fossils can be used as altar objects or charms. Their great age means that they can be used to meditate upon deep time, or to contact very ancient spirits.

Driftwood

My father was an avid collector of driftwood. He would use it for the fire, for household repairs, and would occasionally build furniture out of it, and from an early age I was taught to treasure this gift of the sea. Driftwood may be flotsam or jetsam from ships' cargo, or "natural" wood which has been washed into the sea. My garden altar is a large piece of flat timber found on a beach (and carried home with some difficulty) which must have been cargo at some point in its life.

The beaches of North Devon and Somerset, around the Severn estuary, are especially rich in uncut wood which must have been washed into the sea by the great river Severn. A driftwood wand or staff can be a very effective magical tool. Driftwood can also be used to make charms. A driftwood heart or plaque could have protective symbols carved or burnt into it.

A Driftwood Bullroarer or Spirit Caller

A bullroarer is a flat, oval piece of wood with a long cord threaded through it which, when whirled rapidly in the air makes a deep humming noise. It is used to consecrate a working place and summon spirits.

Driftwood can be used to make an excellent bullroarer. I found a lovely piece of wood which I used to make a bullroarer on a walk along the East Fife coast of Scotland with some witch friends and it has become one of my treasured magical tools.

To make a bullroarer you need a flat piece of driftwood between six and ten inches long. Cut and sand the wood into a smooth, flat oval shape. It should be as thin as you can make it, ideally between and eighth and a quarter of an inch thick, and you will need to keep sanding it until it is completely smooth. Then make a hole in the wood as close as possible to one end. Leave the wood somewhere cool to dry. Driftwood can split as it dries, so I rubbed linseed oil into mine several times whilst it was drying, and let the wood soak up as much oil as it wanted. When the wood is fully dried, polish it to a shine with a soft cloth. The linseed oil should ensure a good shine to the wood, or you can finish it with beeswax. Then thread a strong cord or string, at least six feet long, through the hole in the bullroarer and tie the end very securely. Your bullroarer is ready for use. In a wide open space, twirl the bullroarer above your head rapidly, being very careful to keep it well above you and safely away from anyone else (it could cause serious injury of it hit anybody) and don't let go of it. The bullroarer will make a deep humming, whirring noise which will connect you instantly with the spirit world. Using the bullroarer is a very good way to consecrate a space and begin a ritual. A driftwood bullroarer is especially effective for calling up sea spirits.

Shells

Seashells of many different kinds can be used in magic. Some have obvious magical symbolism. The small cowrie shells which can be found around western coasts and larger spiral conch shells can be used to represent the goddess and are often used on altars. Small boxes covered with shells make good spell boxes, especially if the magic is connected with the sea or sea deities. A shell could be added to a charm to increase its potency.

Sea Glass

Fragments of glass smoothed and etched by the sea can also be used. The beach between Charmouth and Lyme Regis in West Dorset is very rich in tiny fragments of sea glass which I have collected, put into small glass jars and hung up in windows to attract spirits of light and air. Larger single pieces of sea glass can also be bound with wire and used in this way.

Sloe Gin

It might seem strange to include a recipe for sloe gin in a chapter on the sea, but as I always collect my sloes from the cliffs next to a favourite East Devon beach where small blackthorn trees grow in profusion, it seemed appropriate. Sloe gin is a powerful drink and very warming after a winter walk by the sea. It can also be used in the chalice at rituals. It is very easy to make.

To make sloe gin you will need sloes, a bottle of gin, sugar and a large clean jar with a good airtight lid. First collect your sloes. Sloes are the fruit of the blackthorn, one of the great magical trees of Britain They are ready in autumn and should be picked in October, ideally after the first frost. Fresh sloes are very bitter so do not be tempted to snack on them whilst picking. You will need enough sloes to half fill your jar. Make sure the sloes are clean. With a sharp knife, score each sloe several times before putting them in the jar. This will allow the juice to percolate into the gin.

Next, pour a good layer of sugar, about half an inch thick, into the jar. Then fill the jar with gin up to the top and secure the lid tightly. Give the jar a good shake. The red juice of the sloes should begin to seep out into the gin. Now put the jar in a dark dry place (a store cupboard or larder is ideal). This is where your willpower comes in as you need to keep the gin at least two months before using it. Shake the jar once a week. Gradually, the sloe juice and sugar will become completely dissolved in to the gin.

Your sloe gin should be ready by Midwinter and makes a great addition to Yule rituals and feasts. When it is ready, strain the liquid through a sieve and bottle it. The sloes should be discarded at this stage. Sloe gin improves with age, so the longer you keep it, the better.

Mirrors, Light and Reflections

Mirrors have been used since the earliest times to make magic. The first mirrors were reflecting pools of still water. Then came polished metal, rock crystal and eventually glass. Traditionally, mirrors and glass are used to see spirits and for scrying, or divination. Glass and mirrors reflect; they catch light, reflect it back, send it into dark corners, shatter it into tiny fragments of light, refract it into rainbows. Watching how light behaves when it meets a mirror or glass creates a meditative, receptive state in the mind. Small wonder then that glass and mirrors can help us see into the world of spirit.

We have already seen how ordinary mirrors can play an important part in magical work with the moon and the sea. Now we will venture further into the realms of mirrors, reflections and seeing.

One of the most basic and widespread magical uses of the mirror is to reflect back bad or unwanted influences and return them to their sender. Mirrors are used for this purpose throughout the world.

A witch ball is a large silvered reflective glass sphere which is traditionally hung in a window to protect a house and reflect back negative influences or unwanted spirits.

Witch balls can sometimes be seen in old houses in Devon and can still be bought. They are usually silver but blue or green ones can also be found. A large Christmas tree bauble will do the same job. A small handbag mirror can also be placed in a window to reflect back that which is not wanted.

In seaside areas an old green glass fishing net float, hung up in a bag of knotted string will serve the same purpose. Its deep, green, glassy depths will reflect the world of the sea spirits into the room. When I was a child it was still possible to find these treasures of the sea washed up on beaches occasionally and the green glass float that my father and I found on a beachcombing walk over fifty years ago still has pride of place in my front room.

The spirits of the air love reflective glass. Old chandelier pieces can be bought cheaply at car boot sales or antique fairs and hung up in a sunny window. They will refract sunlight around a room, splitting it into intensely coloured, vivid rainbows which will attract spirits and have a deep, calming effect which promotes health and also induces a meditative state. As the rainbows move around the room, you will sense that it is full of spirits. Letting this intense light flow directly over your body is a very powerful magical experience.

In a south-facing window, especially if you live away from bright street lights, chandelier pieces will also reflect the light of the full moon into moonbows, which have subtler colours than sunlight. This is very direct, deep moon magic. Bathe in the moonbows; let them rest on your face and body. Catch a moonbow on your hand and look at it.

A glass bowl or jar filled with coloured glass marbles makes a good home for spirits of light and air.

Marbles can also be placed in small glass jars and hung up in a window. Small jam or yoghourt jars can be used; clear tealight holders will also work well. Twist some wire firmly round the lip of the jar to make a hanger. Glass smoothed by the sea can be collected on a seaside walk and used instead of marbles if you prefer.

74

The spirits attracted by glass and mirrors used in these ways are creatures with a fleeting, excitable presence which is immediately and strongly felt. They foster a very creative magical atmosphere which will help you generate new ideas and inspire you. Beware though: these spirits are very ephemeral and will leave as quickly as they came. You will need to fix what they show you immediately in your memory or record it in your journal.

Here is a simple mirror spell to reflect away and send back negative or unwanted influences. Traditionally, this was often used if a person thought they were being ill-wished, but it can also be used to reflect away anxiety and other problems. I have used it often and find it very effective. Take your mirror and place it in an upright position. Take a candle and a needle; you can choose the colour of the candle according to your purpose. Use the needle to scratch into the candle something that represents what you wish to reflect away. This can be a symbol, a word or an image; keep it simple and focus your intent into it as you scratch it into the candle. Then push the needle right through the candle horizontally, at least half way down the candle, more if you wish.

Put the candle into a holder and place it in front of your mirror. Extinguish all artificial lights. Now light the candle, focusing your intent once more on the purpose of your spell. Leave the candle to burn down undisturbed. As with all spells, forget about it once you have done it so that it can get on with its work undisturbed. Once the candle has burnt down to the needle and the needle has fallen out of it, your spell will be complete.

Scrying

Scrying is an old word which simply means "looking" but it has the magical sense of looking inwards, into the spirit world, and seeing that which cannot be seen in the everyday world. Gazing into a pool of deep, still water is perhaps the most primeval form of scrying. Later came mirrors and crystal balls.

You can scry using a simple large glass bowl filled with water into which black ink has been poured. The darkness of the surface is an important factor in scrying. I have a terracotta mixing bowl with a shiny black, glazed inside which filled with water makes an excellent scrying bowl.

An ordinary mirror may also be used for scrying. It should be cleansed and consecrated to your gods and kept covered, away from prying eyes and used only for magical purposes.

You may wish to use a crystal ball. I am not keen on crystals myself as many are mined in very unethical ways, but if you can source one that you are happy with, then it will make an excellent scrying instrument. Crystal balls are usually made of quartz, but it is also possible to obtain glass ones if you prefer. Always keep your crystal covered and be warned: never leave it in sunlight as crystals concentrate the sun's rays and can cause fires.

One of the most traditional scrying instruments, and the one that I use most frequently is a dark or black mirror. The advantage of this is that you can make it yourself. A dark mirror is simply a sheet of glass with the back painted black. To make your dark mirror you need a piece of glass. This can be any size or shape that you want; convex clock face glass is often used as the rounded surface is preferred to flat glass, but any piece of glass will do. You may want to choose or make a frame for your dark mirror first and then get glass to fit it (much easier than making a frame to fit the glass). Carefully paint one side of the glass black. If you are using a clock glass, paint the concave surface. Water-based emulsion paint is the easiest to use, and dries quickly. The paint should be applied thick and undiluted and you may need to use more than one coat. Ensure that the paint is thick and even and that you cannot see through it. You can leave the mirror as it is, but it is better to put it in a frame. It will be easier to hold, or hang on a wall. Fix the mirror into the frame with the painted side at the back and make a backing for the mirror so that the paint does not scratch. Thick paper or card will be fine for this, or you can use wood.

The dark mirror works better than an ordinary one for scrying as the black surface screens out extraneous reflections and makes concentration easier. Your dark mirror should be consecrated and always kept covered when not in use. A traditional way to consecrate a dark mirror is with the herb mugwort (Artemisia vulgaris) which is sacred to the Moon Goddess and which promotes dreams and visions. Mugwort is a very common herb which grows profusely in hedgerows and it is easy to collect a supply. It has a delicate, cool scent which is redolent of the moon. The Mirror should be rubbed with mugwort before use. Cecil Williamson's own dark mirror is kept in the Museum of Witchcraft in Boscastle and retains a special power and beauty.

Summoning spirits to appear in a mirror is an old, traditional aspect of witchcraft. Scrying is always done at night, with all extraneous artificial light screened out. Always begin by casting a magic circle around you to create a safe working space. Whether you choose to scry with a dark mirror or an ordinary one, the usual method is to sit quietly with your mirror and light one or more candles . Depending on the magical purpose I have in mind, I usually use two candles, one on either side of the mirror. The colours will be chosen according to my magical intention. All other lights will be extinguished. As with all magic making, the work is done slowly and very deliberately so that the will and concentration are increased with every stage of the process. The lighting of the candles may be accompanied either by the speaking of appropriate words or by silently honouring the spirits of the flames and asking them to aid you in your work.

To scry you must be calm and switch off your everyday mind. As with all deep magical work, begin by breathing slowly and deeply, and emptying your mind. Enter the light trance state which is the prerequisite for all focused magical work and concentrate your magical will. Gaze at the surface of the water or mirror for as long as it takes until you go beyond the reflective surface and start to see into the Inner worlds with your mind's eye. In this state you may see spirits, or have visions, or find the answers to questions or problems. Working magic such as this may take a long time. Allow the process to take as long as it needs; do not attempt to rush it or it will not work. Allow the spirit visions to develop in their own time, not yours. You should find that you will be able to remember such visions in great detail and that they will stay in your mind's eye. Scrying is most usually about looking, but you may find that the spirits speak with you. Once you have finished your scrying, thank any spirits that have manifested and ask them respectfully to depart. Then extinguish the candles and close your circle.

As with any spirit work, scrying is serious, advanced magic which should not be attempted until you are confident in your abilities. What appears in your mirror may not be what you expect and you will need to be prepared for this and be able to deal with it. Do not be fearful but keep your magical wits about you. I use scrying only for important magical purposes. Do not trivialise this process. Using it too often, or for very minor things will devalue your magic and can have unpleasant effects. If you treat it lightly, or as a game, so will the spirits and you will not like the results. Always make sure that spirits have been thanked and have departed before you put out your candles and close your circle.

One more thing: if a spirit appears in your mirror, never, ever look behind you or turn around to see what is there.

HeaRth and Home

The witch's home is used for magic more than any other working place. It is full of everyday magic. If you work with spirits, then your home will be their home too. The magic you make in your home will create a pervasive atmosphere which will reflect your magical intentions. Visitors to my home who are unaware that I am a witch often comment on its warm and happy atmosphere. This is, of course, because I cherish the spirits in my home and do everything I can to make them feel welcome and at home. Some of these spirits will create a happy and welcoming atmosphere; others will never reveal anything of themselves to visitors. The witch's home may be home to many spirits of different kinds. Cecil Williamson often told me that all his rather ancient domestic appliances were indwelt by spirits. "Thoughts are things" was one of his favourite sayings. Every day he would respectfully bid good morning to the spirits dwelling in his fridge, washing machine, cooker and vacuum cleaner. After Cecil died, his relatives (who had nothing to do with witchcraft) were mystified to find that the domestic appliances in Cecil's house had all stopped working at once. Plugs and fuses were changed and minor repairs carried out, but it made no difference. The appliances still refused to work despite there being nothing apparently wrong with them. It was obvious to me that the spirits in these machines, lovingly cherished by Cecil over many years, were distressed and angry that no one greeted them anymore, and had withdrawn their labour as a result.

Since the earliest of times, humans have understood that they need to protect the places where they live and have created all manner of charms, spells and other magic to make their homes safe, healthy and happy places. The forms taken by this magic have changed over the centuries and in different cultures but the intentions have not, and it is the intent that matters. When we see an ancient witch bottle, or a child's shoe placed in a chimney, or a sigil over a doorway, we recognise the maker's need to protect their living space and their family.

I have been making my own house charms and spells for many years. Some of them were taught to me by other witches and magicians, some I learnt about through reading and research; others are completely my own invention. You might like to try making some of these things. Equally, I hope that these ideas might inspire you to create your own personal spells and charms. Do remember, that as with all magic making, it is your intent and will that are the most important things. It does not matter too much what the end result looks like, because we are not seeking to create art objects here. You will find, however, that charms created with magical intent will have a real power and authenticity that will surprise and delight you. If you keep on at this, you will find that you develop your own style or "vocabulary" of magic making, and that you will find new and inventive ways of using things to make spells and charms, Let your magical mind and the spirits lead you and this will soon become a central part of your personal witchcraft.

As with tools, altars and other magical objects, do not spend lots of money on expensive materials because that defeats the whole purpose of doing this, which is to practise real witchcraft and not be a passive consumer. With very few exceptions, you should be able to find what you need at very little cost. If something has cost a lot of money, it will occupy a very different place in your mind than something you have made yourself with materials you have found using your own ingenuity. You will find much of what you need in hedgerows and woodland (feathers, nuts, seeds, thorns, cast off sheep's wool for example) but always take only what you need and do not be greedy. If ever you need to take a part of a living plant or tree, do it carefully and ask permission of the spirits. If you do this in the right spirit, you may be given unexpected gifts by the spirits. I once went walking on Dartmoor to gather some rowans and came across a wonderful horned sheep's skull, bleached white by the wind and rain, left right in my pathway. The seashore can provide stones, shells and driftwood and other treasures. Fragments of glass smoothed by the sea, rope, netting and other stuff left by the tides can be used for magic and removing this detritus helps in a small way to repair the damage done to the marine environment by human carelessness.

Other things (bottles, jars, old mirrors) can be bought cheaply at car boot sales and charity shops. When I work with fabric I use odds and ends saved from clothes that have worn out or buy old clothes for pennies at jumble sales. This way I am recycling stuff that would otherwise go to waste as well as finding lovely materials for magical work. Any recycled materials should be cleaned both physically and also psychically before you use them.

A Household Altar

Perhaps the first magical thing that you will want to make or assemble will be an altar to your gods. Household altars or shrines are common in many spiritual traditions. Roman houses always contained altars to the Lares and Penates; the gods and spirits of the household. The Lares were the deities of the house and hearth and their statues or symbols would be placed by the hearth. Incense would be offered to them and they would be decorated with flowers at festivals. The Penates oversaw the production and preservation of food and were honoured in the kitchen and the larder. Hindu houses will usually contain an altar dedicated to Ganesh, Lakshmi or one of the other gods, and many Catholic houses have shrines to the Virgin Mary or one of the saints. Humans like to dedicate a place in their dwellings to the worship of their gods, and witches are no exception.

Witches' household altars are very individual and personal creations which reflect the witch's magical personality and there is no set formula for what one should contain. The household altar should be placed in the North and in a quiet place suitable for honouring the gods and doing magical work. Do not put your altar in a door way or a busy or noisy place where it will be disturbed. Take your time choosing the site for your altar. Place it somewhere which instinctively feels right to you and let the spirits guide you.

A household altar can be very simple but it should always be made with love and respect for the gods. You might use a table to make your altar, or a shelf; use whatever feels right to you. What you place on your altar is entirely up to you. Usually a witch's altar will have objects representing Goddess and God. These might be statues or pictures or the altar might simply contain two stones chosen to represent Goddess and God (a cock rock and a fanny stone as Cecil Williamson called them). A piece of horn or deer antler might also be used to represent the God.

If you are good at carving, sculpting or painting, then you may wish to make your own representations of Goddess and God; if not, then you can easily obtain them. I must admit that when creating my first altar I broke my usual rule of finding and making everything for my magical work as my sculptural skills are non-existent. My household altar contains a small statue of the Goddess Isis which I bought over twenty years ago from a place near the British Museum and have tended lovingly ever since. You may also wish to add items representing the four elements. I have a buzzard's feather for air, a horseshoe for fire, a seashell for water and a quartz stone for earth. All these things were found locally in Devon. Candles and candleholders, and some form of incense burner are also usually present. The candles can be chosen according to the season and your magical intent, and you can, of course, make candles yourself. Salt and water for ritual use are also often kept on the altar.

You may then add other items of personal significance to you. Your altar should reflect the place where you live and work and the things you consider to be most important about you. My altar contains a tiny ship in a bottle which my father made when he was a boy, a crow's skull and a shed deer antler picked up in Ashclyst Forest, a white stone with a red crescent moon mark on it found on the beach at Budleigh Salterton, a very phallic flint from Branscombe beach, a lock of hair from a beloved cat, a bottle of cowrie shells which my brother and I collected when we were children and a tiny brass cauldron picked up at a car boot sale. All these things have personal meanings and significance for me and I use them in magical work. You will find items for your altar gradually, over time. Start with a few things and add gradually. It is good to spend months or years creating your altar and adding the right things as and when you find them, rather than rushing to complete the altar all at once. Let the gods and spirits provide things for you in their own time.

I dress my altar to reflect the changing of the seasons. It might contain first blossoms in spring, flowers in summer, acorns, conkers and fruits in autumn and evergreens and mistletoe in winter. I also use my altar for magical work. Spells and charms and other items made for magic will be placed on the altar once made and left there for a while to ask the blessing of the deities on them. You will find that you instinctively know what to place on your altar.

The altar should always be kept clean and tidy as a mark of respect to the gods. It should never be allowed to get dusty or dirty and flowers and other vegetable material should be removed once they are past their best (unless, of course they are being kept for a magical purpose). Keep your altar fresh; if you have water on the altar, change it frequently; light candles and incense regularly and bring new flowers, fruit or other offerings. The household altar will become the living heart of your magical home and should always be tended and respected as such. When you make magic using physical objects (charms, spells etc), these things can be placed on the altar for a while so that your gods can bless them and give them an extra magical charge before they find their way in the world.

The Heaꞧth

At a very early stage in our evolution, humans learnt to control fire and use it to provide warmth and cook food. We honour fire for the gifts it brings us and respect its power and attendant dangers. Since the earliest time the fire-place or hearth has been a vital site of magical activity. Many ancient Pagan traditions honoured deities of the hearth: Hestia in Rome and Hertha in the Northern European traditions are two examples, and the spirits of the ancestors were also often honoured at the hearth. Many traditional magical objects such as witch bottles and protection charms were placed in the hearth or chimney and it was traditionally a place which needed to be honoured and protected. It was also thought of as a place where the power of fire would heighten the effect of magic worked there. Until the Industrial Revolution, food was cooked and water boiled over open fires so the bubbling cauldron or cook pot hanging in the hearth would have been a normal part of everyday life.

I have always chosen to live in houses with a "real" fire and would find it very difficult to be without one. For sure, a real fire demands a lot more effort than instant central heating at the press of a button, but for me it is an important part of my magical life. I am lucky to have an inglenook fireplace and, yes, there is an old, blackened cauldron hanging over it. I can choose what kind of wood to burn for specific magical outcomes, burn incense on the fire, make spells which involve burning or singeing objects and brew herbs in my cauldron. I know it is not always possible to have real fires in these days of urban living but, if you can manage it, an open hearth fire or wood burning stove can be an important working place.

My hearth contains a number of charms. Some of them are works in progress, placed there to strengthen them before they move on to other places and people. Some of them live there permanently, protecting the house and its inhabitants. There is a circle of witch stones, threaded on wire and hung in the chimney, a witch bottle going quietly about its business, a small charm box which was the first thing brought into the house when I moved here and a thick plait of red wool made during a ritual for me when I was ill as a curing spell.

Spirit jars and houses

I learnt how to make Devon spirit jars and houses from Cecil Williamson. Cecil had several of these in his Museum of Witchcraft and would occasionally come across them in old houses. Over the years I have taken what Cecil taught me and adapted it so that it works for me. These spirit jars and houses are quite different in form and intent from the Chinese spirit houses which can be bought commercially.

A Devon Spirit Jar

For this you need a glass jar. Size and shape are up to you. You could use something as simple as a jam jar. I like to make my spirit jars quite large and find old sweet jars, which often turn up at car boot sales, are perfect for this purpose. Bottles are also fine, provided they have a fairly wide neck. The jar should have a lid or some kind of stopper (or you can make one) which will keep the contents dry and free from dust. The jar should be washed thoroughly until it is squeaky clean and shiny and it should be absolutely dry inside before you use it. This is all part of respecting the spirits.

To make your empty jar into a spirit jar, you are going to put into it things that spirits like. When I first did this I worked with the things that Cecil Williamson taught me about but over the years I have let the spirits guide me and used the things they have told me they want. Traditional Devon items to put in a spirit jar include small quartz pebbles, little seashells (cowries and pink "fairy toenails" are good), feathers, bits of mirror and glass worn smooth by the sea, ears of barley or wheat and a piece of red wool or thread with nine knots in it. Of course, you should gather these things yourself. Don't just follow this list of ingredients; listen to the spirits and use what feels right to you. Avoid anything that will rot or perish and dry any animal or vegetable materials thoroughly before using them.

Your jar should be not more than a quarter full of these things as you need to leave plenty of room for the spirits. When you have filled the jar to your satisfaction, seal it carefully and put it in a nice warm, comfortable place in your house. It should not be anywhere too conspicuous where visitors might notice it, as it will want to work its magic quietly, and it should not be in direct sunlight. Don't shut it away in a cupboard or other completely dark place.

Now you have to invite a spirit to live in your jar. Empty your mind of all everyday thoughts and focus on your magical will. Think of the kind of spirit you would like to live in your jar. What sort of qualities should it have? What would you like it to bring to your home and your life? Then very quietly and with completely focused intent, invite the spirit in. Once it has taken up residence you may notice changes inside the jar and you will sense a difference in the atmosphere of your home.

You must cherish the spirit once it has come to live with you. Greet it every day, talk with it regularly and listen to what it tells you. If the spirit tells you its name, never speak it aloud. Always keep the spirit jar clean and tidy and look after it well. Never let it get dusty or neglected. Spirits which are invited guests are not bound by physical matter so the spirit jar is a living space within your home and a place to rest which the spirit may visit and use as it pleases. If you treat the spirit kindly and respectfully (just as you would wish to be treated) it will make its home in the jar and live there permanently. If you neglect it, it will manifest its unhappiness in some tangible way and probably leave.

You can vary the contents of your spirit jar according to the kind of spirit you wish to attract to your home. A jar full of crow feathers or a bird's skull would attract a very different kind of spirit from one full of shiny glass and quartz pebbles. Any material can be used if it is right for your purpose.

A Spirit House

This is a resting place for the spirits who are around your house. You do not need to attract a specific spirit to it; it is for those who are already there. It will feel very different in character to a spirit jar, much more open and "edgy". Nothing about this kind of spirit house is straight or logical; this is its

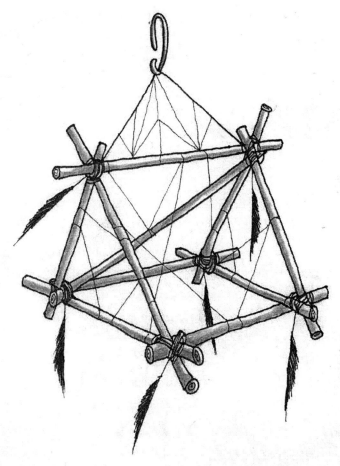

most important characteristic and it is what the spirits like
about it.

To make a spirit house you will need hawthorn twigs, black
wool or thread, and small dark feathers (hawk or rooks'
feathers are ideal but use whatever suits you best). Make the
twigs into an irregular structure, joining them together with
the wool or thread. Some sides should have three corners or

joins, others four or five. The important thing is that you should not make a regular shape; twigs, sides and edges should be of different lengths. Bind the joins together firmly with the wool or thread, concentrating with your magical mind as you do so. Next with more thread, bind feathers into the joins. Then use your remaining thread to make a lattice or net between the twigs, twining it round them and weaving it through them to make it secure. Finally make a hanging loop for your spirit house and hang it high up in a quiet corner of your house (the kitchen is best) where it is unlikely to be noticed except by spirits. Unlike the spirit jar, the spirit house should not be cleaned. If it attracts cobwebs and dust, so much the better. You will find after a while that you are able to detect the presence of spirits around the spirit house. You may notice a dark, focused energy. Always remember to acknowledge, honour and respect these spirits.

Witch Bottles

Witch bottles are a very old, traditional form of protective magic in Devon, just as they are in many parts of the country. They are sometimes found in old houses, usually hidden in a chimney or built into a wall or roof space where prying eyes will not see them. They have a strong magic all of their own.

The original purpose of witch bottles was to repel bad magic or return it to its sender. They were used by cunning men and women to out-nasty bad intent and send it packing. A person who had been the victim of a curse or bad magic would visit the cunning man or woman and be told to make a witch bottle. The contents would be deliberately revolting, because like would, in this instance, repel like. I heard recently of a research chemist who analysed the contents of 17th century witch bottles found in old houses in the midlands. He had to do this with great care because the contents were still noxious after four centuries. A traditional witch bottle would be made

91

of glass and have a good, airtight stopper or cork. It would be filled with pins, rusty nails, thorns and the urine of the bewitched person who would take it home and place it in their chimney. When the fire was lit it would heat up the contents of the bottle, causing pain to the person who had cast the original spell. This would mean either that the originator of the bad magic would be discovered and called to account, or that the pain would cause them to call off their spell or curse. More recently witch bottles have been used as general protective magic. They are extremely effective at repelling spells, curses and other bad intentions, and are also used to repel unwanted spirits.

You can make a very effective witch bottle by filling it with thorns, pins and rusty nails and then topping it up with your urine, but if you don't want to go the whole hog and pee into the bottle, there is a less noxious alternative.

Fill a glass bottle with pins, nails and thorns and instead of urine, top it up with red wine or vinegar. You may wish to add a few protective herbs of your own choosing. This will work well as a protective spell if you do it with concentrated magical intent. Seal the bottle tightly using melted wax around the stopper as a final touch. The bottle should then be hidden somewhere dark and private in your house. Please don't put it in a prominent place and point it out proudly to all your visitors as it is unlikely to work if you do that. It could be built into a wall, hidden in a chimney (but not in a place where it will get too hot and explode), cellar or roof space, put under the stairs or the sink or at the back of a dark cupboard. Usually you will know instantly when you have found the right place as the bottle will lead you to it. The point is that it should be somewhere where you can't see it, and it should be left to get on with its magic quietly and undisturbed. If you move house, don't be tempted to take the witch bottle with you. You made it for a specific place and it should stay there. You can always make another one for your new home.

Another kind of witch bottle is used to protect a place from unwanted spirit attention by distracting or confusing the spirits. This kind of bottle is filled with hundreds or thousands of short pieces of thread of many different colours. It should be packed absolutely full of threads and then sealed. The spirits will be distracted by the brightly coloured threads and leave your place alone. I make bottles like this using the offcuts and ends of threads from my knitting, sewing and embroidery. Every time I finish a piece of thread I put the end into a bottle. Of course, most of my knitting and sewing has a magical purpose and every single piece of thread which goes into the bottle is imbued with my magical intent and energy. These bottles can take months or years to complete. When the bottle is packed tightly full of threads and I can't stuff anymore in, it is sealed and finished with wax. Unlike "pin" witch bottles, a thread bottle can be placed somewhere visible. I like to put thread bottles on a mantel piece or in a window where their "attract and distract" effect can be maximised.

I have also created a third kind of witch bottle which I like to give as a gift or use if I am asked to perform protective magic for other people. It is designed as gentle protective magic for a house and its inhabitants. I sometimes get asked to help when a house has a bad atmosphere, or where people have had a run of bad luck or are unhappy, and I find that this kind of witch bottle helps the magic along in a positive way.

As with the other kinds of witch bottle, for this you need a glass bottle with a good strong cap or stopper. The bottle should be clean and dry. You will also need any or all of the following:

• Salt

• Pins

• Dried rowan berries

• Dried protective herbs (of your choice)

- Dried flower petals (of your choice)
- Dried seeds (of your choice)
- Dried chillies

Make sure that any plant material you use is completely dried as otherwise your bottle may go mouldy.

Fill the bottle, placing layers of different materials into it (for example a layer of pins, then a layer of salt, then a layer of rose petals). Salt is used because it is a great cleanser and purifier. Pins will repel and protect. Different flower and plant materials will be used for their specific magical qualities. Pack each layer of material down as tightly as you can before adding the next one. I use the handle of a wooden spoon to ram the material down as tightly as possible.

Your aim should be to pack as much into the bottle as you possibly can until absolutely nothing more can be fitted into it. Then seal your bottle and finish it with wax. As with all other magical work, you can complete the process by saying an appropriate charm or spell, or by silently focusing your magical intent on the work in hand. When it is finished, your bottle should resemble one of those bottles of layers of different coloured sand which used to be popular tourist souvenirs years ago.

Choose the contents of this kind of bottle according to your magical purpose. For a house which has a cold or forbidding atmosphere you might make a "hot" witch bottle consisting of layers of red and orange materials and things associated with warmth and the sun such as dried rowan berries, the petals of marigolds or other red or orange flowers, and chillies, interspersed with layers of salt. In addition to purifying, the white salt will accentuate the colours of your other materials.

A bottle to promote a sense of calm wellbeing and assist the inhabitants of a house in positive magical work might contain layers of rose petals, mugwort and rosemary as well as salt.

Once you grasp the principle of this you will invent your own combinations of materials for your magical work. You can use anything that makes sense to you. This kind of witch bottle, which is made for other people, should look good as well as having a strong purpose. The user of the bottle should place it somewhere out of direct sunlight and away from heat and damp, but where it will be seen. It will act as a morale booster and the user will be able to look at it and appreciate it as it does its magical work.

Rowan

The rowan tree, sometimes called mountain ash, is one of the great magical trees. It likes poor soil and high ground and grows in the high, wild wet places that other trees shun. It is found on mountains and moorland and is held to be sacred throughout the western and northern parts of Britain. It is particularly revered in Devon, where it grows in profusion on Dartmoor and Exmoor. It can often be found growing out of cracks between boulders; there are some particularly fine rowans by the Tolmen stone which seem to grow straight out of stone with no earth to hold them.

The rowan is a small tree and on the high moors is often bent and twisted by the wind; white blossoms in spring are followed by masses of bright red berries. In Devon these appear around Lammas and last on the high ground until after the Autumn Equinox. Rowan berries can be an extraordinary sight; I once walked from Two bridges to Wistman's Wood on Dartmoor on a wild, wet August day. As I walked, the rain became torrential and the sky turned dark as night. Suddenly, a rowan tree came into my view over the brow of a hill. Its red berries were so bright against the black sky that they looked as if they were tiny electric lights. It was an unforgettable sight; a gift from the Old Ones.

Rowan is the great protective tree. Its wood and berries are used to make all kinds of charms which will protect the user against all harm, and especially against sorcery. The berries are bright red, the colour of blood and life. Red is very commonly used in charms for strength and protection. Rowan was always used to protect houses and farms and I still occasionally come across rowan berries or wood hung up in a lambing shed or barn to keep the animals safe. The old carters would tie rowan twigs or crosses into their horses' manes to protect them. Rowan was also held to be a protection against lightning strikes and in Devon and Cornwall it was kept on ships to protect against storms.

A rowan tree is essential in a witch's garden. It is a small tree which won't take up much room and dwarf varieties can be obtained which will grow happily in pots. You can often tell a Devon witch's house by the rowan tree planted close to the door. It is an easy tree to grow as it thrives on neglect. Don't fuss over a rowan; let it be itself.

There are many charms that can be made from rowan wood and berries; here are some which I have made and used. There is an old Devon tradition that rowan wood or berries should always be gathered from a tree the witch has never visited before. This is easy to do on Dartmoor or Exmoor as there are so many of them. When gathering rowan wood or berries, take only what you need. Always leave plenty of berries for the birds, who love them and thank the spirit of the tree for its gift.

Rowan wood is full of water. It is easy to remove the bark with your fingers (a knife is not necessary) and the wood beneath requires little smoothing or finishing. Rowan wood should be left somewhere cool and dry to season for several months before you use it so that it does not split as it dries out. The pale wood turns a beautiful golden colour when dried.

Please make sure when you are gathering rowan berries that children are not allowed to eat the fresh berries as they can be poisonous to small stomachs in their fresh state.

Hidden on a ledge above my front door is a peeled, smooth rowan stick gathered from a special working place on Dartmoor. I used a wood burning tool to incise protective symbols on the stick. You could just as easily use ink or paint if you prefer. I used some of the traditional protective symbols of witchcraft.

I then wrote I AM ROWAN and the name of the working place where the stick was found. I used the Coel Brenin magical alphabet as I like to use magical rather than everyday letters when making magic. You could use Runes, Ogham, Theban script, Enochian, or any magical alphabet which feels right to you. The stick was then blessed on my altar and put in its hiding place above the door to protect my house.

Another protective charm which is widely used is the rowan cross. These small charms were often carried in the pockets of farmers or shepherds or hung up in farm buildings to protect animals. The rowan cross is very easy to make. It consists of two small rowan twigs of equal length bound together with red thread.

The equal armed cross is a symbol which is much older than Christianity. It can be found carved on Neolithic passage graves and has been used for thousands of years. It symbolises the four cardinal directions and the four elements with you at the centre, the solar year, and the union of male (the vertical axis) and female (the horizontal axis).

When making your rowan cross, be mindful that it is the act of binding the twigs with red thread which is the expression of your magical intent. Do this purposefully, concentrating your mind on the idea of protection as you go. You can, of course, speak a protective spell as you do it. One very traditional one is: " Rowan tree and red thread, put the witches to their speed", or "Rowan tree and red thread, make the witches flee in dread" There are lots of local variations of this rhyme.

Witch posts were usually made from rowan wood in the western and northern parts of Britain. A witch post is a wooden post carved with an equal-armed cross, hearts and other traditional "witch signs" and placed either next to the door of a house or in the chimney place where it would prevent witches or evil spirits from passing through the house. I have a fine witch post in my chimney place, carved by a Cornish magician. It sits quietly behind the fire, unnoticed by most people, working its magic.

Rowan berries can be used as a protective charm. Gather fresh rowan berries and use a needle to string them onto a length of red thread. Always use an odd number of berries. Hang your string of berries somewhere warm, dark and dry for a couple of months until they are dry. Don't hang them in the light as this will cause them to lose their colour. When the berries are completely dry, tie the two ends of the thread together to form a circle. Make sure that you do this with magical intent. The circle of rowan berries can be carried in the pocket or hung up somewhere for protection.

Loose rowan berries can be dried and used in charm bags, or witch bottles, or as a constituent of incense.

Rowan berries can be made into a delicious jelly. This tastes a little like cranberry jelly but with a darker, smoky taste all of its own. It makes an excellent part of a magical feast, especially at Midwinter, and is delicious with many savoury dishes such as roast potatoes, cheese and meats. It is a great witch's delicacy.

To make rowan jelly you will need:

• A quantity of rowan berries (about half a carrier bag full)

• Lemons

• Sugar

• A preserving pan or, if you don't have one, the largest pan you can find

• A jelly bag or a large piece of muslin (big enough to contain your rowan berries)

• A large bowl

• A large measuring jug

• Clean jam jars with lids

Pick your rowans when they are ripe and fresh. Wash the rowan berries and pick all the stems off them (this is the tedious bit). Make sure you remove all the stems; if you leave them on the berries they will make your jelly bitter.

Put the rowans in your pan and cover them with water. Bring the pan to the boil then turn the heat right down and simmer the berries gently until about half the liquid has evaporated.

Put the berries into the jelly bag or muslin and hang it over the large bowl. If using muslin you will need to tie it up to make a bag. Let the liquid drip into the bowl until only the berries remain in the bag. Do not be tempted to hasten this process by squeezing the berries as this will make the jelly cloudy.

Pour the liquid into the measuring jug. For each pint (about 575 ml) of liquid you will need the juice of one lemon and one pound (500 grams) of sugar. Squeeze the appropriate number of lemons. Now you need to sterilise your jam jars. Remove the lids and put them in the oven on a very low heat. By the time you have made your jelly they will be sterilised.

Now put the liquid, lemon juice (make sure there are no pips in it) and sugar into the pan. Turn the heat up as high as you can and stir it as it is heating up until all the sugar has dissolved. Allow the mixture to boil rapidly (jam makers call this a "rolling boil"). The aim is to get the mixture really hot so that it will set. Stir it frequently to that it does not burn or stick to the pan. The mixture will soon get very hot and start to thicken.

If you have a jam making thermometer, the jelly will reach its setting point at 220 degrees. If you don't, put a couple of saucers in your fridge, When the mixture starts to thicken, put a few drops onto one of the cold saucers and put it in the fridge for a few seconds. Push the edge of your blob of jelly with your finger. If it wrinkles, it has set; if it is still smooth and liquid, it hasn't. You may need to repeat this procedure several times until you are satisfied that your jelly has set. Remove the pan from the heat and allow it to cool for a few minutes. While it is doing this, skim off any scum that may have appeared on the top of the jelly. After the jelly has cooled a little, take your sterilised jars out of the oven and pour the jelly into them and seal the jars tightly.

I usually keep my rowan jelly until Midwinter before using it, or giving it as presents to friends.

Hearts

The heart as a symbol and talisman has been used in witchcraft since ancient times. It has rather fallen out of use in Britain in recent times, and become over-identified with the twee and the folksy. This is a pity because it is a symbol full of magical meaning which can be used to great effect. In many traditions across the world, for example Voudoun and Santeria, the heart is still a vital part of magic.

In the Greek Orthodox tradition of Christianity votive plaques are hung in churches to increase the efficacy of prayers and the flaming heart is one of the most frequently used.

All over the world, the heart is readily understood as a symbol not just of love, but also of abundance, health and good fortune. When we see a heart we instinctively get these meanings, without needing complex verbal explanations. In Voudoun and also in ancient Rome, the symbol of a heart divided into squares, with a dot in the centre of each square was used. This meant that there was room in this heart for everyone. In Voudoun it was used in Veves (sacred drawings) for the goddess of love and sexuality, Erzulie. It meant that Erzulie had infinite room in her heart, and also had the connotation that she could be sexually available to everyone. In Roman cities the same symbol was used as the sign for a brothel.

In the home, the heart is also the symbol of the centre, the beating heart of the life of the place and all that flows from that. Not all traditional uses of the heart are loving or romantic; sometimes it is used in a darker way. Cecil Williamson found instances of sheep's hearts stuck with pins and placed in chimneys as protective charms, keeping harm away from the centre of the home.

I work a lot with the heart and use it in a wide range of ways. A fabric heart, which can be made from scraps of material, stuffed with dried herbs, can be used to drive out malign influences and bring about positive results. This could be used for something very practical: a heart stuffed with southern-wood, camphor and rue will keep moths away from clothes but made magically will work on a subtle as well as a practical level. A heart hung up by the bed and filled with rose petals, mugwort and lavender will drive away nightmares and promote good dreams. Hops will promote sleep. A heart filled with marigold petals, lemon verbena or other herbs of the sun will promote warmth and health. To make a simple fabric heart, cut out two identical heart shapes from fabric of your choice and sew them together, leaving about a centimetre seam allowance. I do this by hand rather than using a sewing machine as each stitch is used to emphasise my magical intent. Leave about an inch of the seam unstitched, stuff the herbs into the heart, then stitch up the remaining seam. Attach a loop of thread to hang the heart by.

An old Devon tradition was the making of a heart-shaped pincushion for a sweetheart. The pincushion would be made of red fabric, usually velvet, and pins would then be stuck into it spelling out the initials of the lovers and symbols of their love for each other. I made one of these pincushions for the Museum of Witchcraft at Boscastle and have made several as gifts for friends' weddings or civil partnership ceremonies. Pincushions are made in the same way as the fabric hearts above but I use wool or kapok rather than herbs for the stuffing so that the pins will stay in permanently.

I have also adapted the pincushion technique and made black felt hearts into which I then push pins in the shape of signs for the horned god or moon goddess. These can be used as altar objects. They are also closer in intention to Cecil Williamson's pin-stuffed sheeps' hearts (as a sensitive vegetarian I couldn't bring myself to use a recently deceased sheep's heart!) and could be used for similar magical purposes.

This embroidered house protection and happiness charm combines the heart with old Pennsylvania Dutch hex patterns and stars. The unwanted and negative spirits and influences will get lost or confused in the concentric triangles. The stars are for Goddess and spirit. The hearts are for love, happiness, health and abundance and the dots are seeds and potential.

The charm is simple to make. You will need some fabric (the type and colour are up to you), embroidery thread and two rowan twigs (or other wood if you prefer). Draw your pattern onto the fabric before you start to sew using a sewing pencil or tailor's chalk. Then embroider your pattern using a simple running stitch or back stitch. Threads of a different colour can be woven through the stitches if you wish. The dots in the hearts can be made using French knots or by sewing two small stitches on top of each other. When you are satisfied with your design, trim the fabric and hem the edges. Attach the rowan twigs to the top and bottom of the fabric so that it will hang properly and make a hanging loop with some embroidery thread and attach it to the top rowan twig.

The heart has become an important element in my vocabulary of magical symbols, so I might combine it with other images or objects to reinforce or add to its meanings. Recently I have made wooden hearts hung with witch stones and painted black or red, or inscribed with other signs such as the sunwheel or the horned god sign. Experimenting and building up a repertoire of personal symbols and images is a key part of this kind of practical magic-making.

Hanòs

The hand is another old protective magical symbol which I like to incorporate into my work. A hand with the palm facing outwards and the fingers upright repels that which is not wanted; it pushes it away. Conversely, a hand with the fingers outstretched may welcome, entice and say "come hither". Hand symbols used to be found in the windows of the old Devon witches. Cecil Williamson collected a beautiful ceramic one from a lady in Sidmouth in East Devon. The lady was a consulting witch who had a lot of local clients. There was a red heart painted in the centre of the palm of the hand. When the witch was in and receiving clients the heart would face outwards in her window; when she was not "open for business" the hand was turned around so the heart could not be seen.

In some middle eastern countries Hand of Fatima talismans are hung up for protection. The horned hand or mano cornuta with the index and little finders pointing upwards and the other fingers made into a fist signifies the horned god and is an old witch sign. Witches may use it as a sign of recognition or wear it as jewellery but do beware, because in Italy, Spain and some other Mediterranean countries it signifies a cuckold and will be taken as a great insult if made to a man. The *mano in fica* ("fig hand"), where the fingers are made into a fist with the tip of the thumb protruding between the index and middle fingers is a sign of the goddess (being reminiscient of the clitoris) and may be worn by witches.This is also an old witch sign and a common protective amulet in Spain and Italy. Beautiful jet ones are made in Santiago da Compostela in Northern Spain.

I like to combine hands and hearts and make hand charms with a heart in the centre of the palm. These may be embroidered onto fabric or painted or burnt into wood. A very effective charm plaque can be made using an old tomato puree tube. This is a neat, if slightly fiddly, piece of magical recycling. Tomato puree tubes are made of soft, malleable metal which is easy to work. When the tomato puree tube is empty (this doesn't work if you roll the tube up when you use it) cut it with strong scissors to remove the top and the bottom and then cut along one side so that you can open it out into a flat piece of metal. One side will be golden coloured (this will form the front of your plaque) and the other will have the painted tube design on it (this will be the back of your plaque). Wash away any tomato residue, being careful not to cut yourself on any jagged edges. Then fold the edges down to the back of the plaque to make a narrow "seam", getting rid of any sharp edges. If the plaque has folds or creases flatten them out with a rolling pin. Draw your design on the back of the plaque with a waterproof felt tip pen. When you are satisfied with it, using a metal knitting needle, an old biro or some other pointed implement, score over your drawing on the back of the plaque into the metal and it will appear in relief on the front. Make a small hole at the top of the

plaque for a hanger and stick a piece of paper or card over the back to finish it.

Tip: if you are not confident of your drawing abilities, use your own hand as a template and draw round it. This will also make the work more personal.

Wreaths and Circles

A wreath is a small circle; traditionally wreaths have been made to celebrate marriages, crown winners and commemorate the dead. The circle has no beginning or ending, so it is an appropriate symbol for these events.

For witches, the circle is the sacred space, apart from ordinary space and time, that we create to worship our gods and work magic in. it is also for us a model of our universe, describing the circles of death and rebirth, the cycles of the moon, sun and seasons, and much more. Small wonder then that wreaths are used in magic-making in many ways.

Wreaths made of seasonal vegetation can be used to decorate ritual spaces and working places. At Beltane a wreath of spring flowers and young oak leaves would be used, at Midsummer a wreath of roses, at Lammas a wreath of ripe corn and ivy leaves bound with red thread, and at Midwinter a wreath of holly, mistletoe, laurel and other evergreens. Ritual wreaths can be placed on an altar or hung on a staff. They are usually made very simply of vegetation twined and tied together and are either burnt or returned to the earth after use. Wreaths of flowers, herbs and leaves may also be made to crown couples at Handfastings or witches' weddings.

More permanent wreaths can be made as magical objects for the home. The usual way to make a wreath base is to use willow or vine branches woven together and tied if necessary.

It is possible to buy readymade wreath bases from florists, but making your own is better. I have a neighbour who is happy to let me prune his willow hedge and keep the offcuts. Willow or vine branches should be used when they have just been cut and are still flexible, before the wood dries out and hardens. Once you have made your wreath base you can weave or tie all kinds of things into it.

A wreath made of birds' feathers fixed to a willow base is one of my treasured magical items. The feathers were collected over a long period of time on walks in the woods and on the Moor. This wreath contains feathers from many different birds including buzzards, owls and ravens. It is used for flying magic and work with spirit birds.

A wreath made from blown eggshells which are then batik dyed is a great magical decoration for Spring Equinox. It is also a major undertaking. The eggs have to be blown, which can be a difficult business. You will need at least seven hen's eggs to make a small circle. Make a pinhole at each end of the egg and gently blow the contents out into a bowl until the egg is empty. This is a painstaking procedure (expect some failures) but you will have plenty of eggs for cooking at the end of it. Each egg is then painted with magical designs using liquid hot wax applied very thinly with a small paint brush or a pin, and immersed in cold water dye. You can purchase this from art and craft suppliers. The dye will "take" on the areas without wax leaving the waxed areas pale. Then the wax is very gently scraped away. Finally thread the dyed eggs onto thin wire using a long needle or bodkin. This is a tricky procedure but well worth the effort. If you can't bear the thought of working with thin, breakable eggshells, you can use the polystyrene eggs available from craft shops but you will need to paint them rather than dyeing them. I made a fragile eggshell wreath for the Museum of Witchcraft at Boscastle in Cornwall and was amazed to find that it survived the devastating flood there in 2004, when many more robust items were destroyed.

Rowan berries can be picked in August and added to a willow or vine wreath base. They can be used fresh or left to dry. Freshly picked conkers which have not yet hardened can be threaded onto wire and made into a wreath for Autumn Equinox. Simply poke holes through the conkers with an old knitting needle or similar implement and thread them onto the wire. Small apples threaded onto wire and made into a wreath can be used as part of Samhain celebrations and eaten by the assembled company.

For sea magic, collect seashells, driftwood, dried seaweed and sea-smoothed glass and stick them onto a willow or vine wreath base (a hot glue gun works well for this). Small witch stones threaded into wire and twisted into a wreath (as mentioned in The Sea chapter) make a wonderful protection charm.

For a kitchen wreath, thread fresh chillies onto thin wire and form them into a circle. Hang the wreath somewhere dark until the chillies have dried so that they keep their bright colour. Ever since chillies first reached Europe they have been used in folk magic to promote health and warmth and strength. This is a good example of the Doctrine of Signatures in magical work (the chillies look and taste hot, so they will bring heat and zest). When working with chillies do remember that they can burn the skin. Wash your hands thoroughly afterwards and don't put your fingers in your mouth or rub your eyes while working with them.

I make wreaths using strips of recycled fabric and fabric hearts which make good magical gifts. I use brightly coloured scraps of fabric; worn out clothes and jumble sale finds are ideal. Bits of old sheets and other plain fabrics can also be easily dyed and added to the mix so that you have plenty of fabric to choose from. I find that similarly coloured fabrics (reds, oranges and pinks, for example, or blues and greens) work best. A completely black wreath, using different textures of fabric looks spectacular.

To make a fabric and heart wreath you will need:

• A willow or vine wreath base

• Scraps of fabric in colours of your choice

• At least seven fabric hearts (see section on hearts for how to make these)

Cut your fabric scraps into strips about an inch wide and six inches long. You will need lots and lots of these. Tie your strips of fabric to the wreath base leaving long "tails" hanging down until it is completely covered (the shaggier the better) and none of the base is showing. Then attach your fabric hearts to the wreath using a needle and embroidery thread.

Finally, make a hanger with a spare strip of fabric. A bright red or blue and green wreath makes a beautiful house charm. Made with magical intent, it will promote happiness and wellbeing. A black wreath with black hearts and small witch stones added is a potent magical item.

A willow or vine wreath base can also be completely wrapped using fabric strips. Knot each strip of fabric around the wreath base, leaving the knot at the front, until none of the base is showing. Then trim the ends of each fabric strip just above the knot. A fabric heart or witch stone or other charm can then be tied onto the bottom of the wreath. A small wreath base about four inches (10cm) in diameter works well. Use a colour appropriate to your magical purpose: red for health and vitality, green for fertility etc. A small wreath wrapped entirely in black fabric (old black T-shirt material is ideal) and hung with a small heart pincushion embellished with a symbol of your choice makes a good banishing charm.

Kitchen charms

There are many charms that can be made with simple household ingredients and you can find the magic in everyday things and deploy it to good advantage in your home. Witches have always done this. In the kitchen and the larder charms ensure that food will be kept safe and cooking will be a fulfilling and successful activity.

Traditionally, charms in the kitchen were used to ensure that the bread rose, that milk and butter did not curdle, that fruit and vegetables were safely preserved and that flour was kept free from weevils. Whilst the fridge has taken over some of these functions, kitchen charms work a quiet magic and if you get this right, they will have an easygoing, effortless presence which will enrich those everyday domestic activities which are the basis of a good life.

Special fruits and herbs have been used over the centuries to create charms, As we have already seen, chillies are used to promote warmth and well being. Chillies are fairly easy to grow on a sunny windowsill, or a greenhouse if you have one. When ripe and red the fruits can be strung onto a thread and hung up to dispel cold and negativity.

A lemon stuck with pins and left somewhere warm to dry also makes a good kitchen charm. Take a fresh lemon and stick it all over with pins. I use ones with coloured glass heads. Let the lemon dry naturally in a warm, dark place; with time it will go rock hard and black. Stand the lemon in a conspicuous place in your kitchen. I have one on a shelf where it does its work quietly, absorbing negative influences.

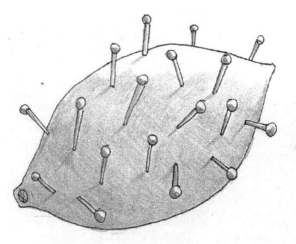

Garlic also has good protective properties. It is easy to grow: just plant single cloves in ordinary soil or a large pot outside in March and by late summer you should have your own stock of garlic bulbs. You can plait these into strings and hang them up. You can also make a kitchen charm bag filled with dried garlic cloves, chillies and dried herbs of your choice. I like to use lemon verbena, lemon balm or marigold petals.

When making kitchen charms, let your magical imagination guide you and find ingredients which have meaning for you. When I moved house some years ago, I found the house I wanted to live in and in order to make sure I got it I left a few grains of rice in the kitchen when I visited it with the estate agent. This was a spell of my own which just came to me when I needed it. A similar local tradition is to scatter a few leek seeds in the garden. You will discover that charm making possibilities are endless and that you will build up your own range of ingredients that have meaning and purpose for you.

Thꞃeaꝺs

This chapter is about operative magic and now we come to spell making. This is apparently everyday, magic but it can have profound effects. When I am asked to work magic, I will most usually create a spell which involves making something physical, because it is the act of making without words, and with concentrated magical intent which will make the magic work. Over many years I have learned how to work with thread and fabric and these are my preferred materials. You could equally work with wood, clay, metal, or whatever you feel an affinity with. I like knitting, sewing, plaiting and knotting, not only because they are activities which humans (and especially women) have been practising since the earliest times, but also because they are simple, repetitive activities which have a deep, meditative quality to them. Knitting in particular induces a light trance state which is very conducive to the practice of magic. Spinning wool with a simple drop spindle and watching the cloud of amorphous fleece form into a thread as one works is also a very magical activity. Learning to use a drop spindle is quite easy and you can acquire unspun fleece or just collect cast off sheep's wool from fences and hedges. This can easily be twisted into a thread with your fingers if you do not wish to use a spindle. Using thread you have spun yourself will increase the magical power of things you make with it.

Tying knots in thread or cord is a very old form of witch magic and covens may work complex spells which involve the whole group working in a circle tying complex knots as magic is worked. Special forms of knotting specific to the witch's tradition may be used. Cecil Williamson recorded Cornish witches at Boscastle "selling the wind" to sailors. They would tie three knots in a piece of rope. The sailors could untie one knot to produce a breeze, two knots untied would produce a stronger wind and three something approaching a gale. An old and very widespread spell is worked by making nine knots in

113

a piece of string or thread. I usually use red wool for this. Red is my preferred colour because it signifies blood, fire, energy and life, but I may vary this according to my magical purpose. Cut a piece of wool or other thread about a yard (or metre) long. Concentrate deeply on the purpose of the spell. Then make nine knots in the thread, speaking this old spell as you go:

By knot of one the spell's begun

By knot of two it cometh true

By knot of three so mote it be

By knot of four the open door

By knot of five the spell's alive

By knot of six my spell I fix

By knot of seven the gates of heaven

By knot of eight the open gate

By knot of nine the thing is mine!"

There are many variants of this rhyme. The knotted thread may be kept safe somewhere, hung up or given to the person it was made for, according to your purpose.

Plaiting is another very effective way to make a spell. Like knotting, it is an ageless, repetitive action which can be used to focus and intensify magical intent, and it is something most people learn to do at an early age. Plaiting is based around the number three, which makes it ideal for magic. The number three is special to witches in many ways. It puts us in mind of the triple Goddess (Maiden, Mother and Hag) and tradition specifies that magic is stronger if the number three is incorporated into it, so that things are done three times. A plait will be an expression of the number three and its magical strength. Three threads, or multiples of three, are plaited together and the purpose of the spell is repeated over and over until all of the thread is plaited. A knot is then tied at the end and the intent sealed into the plait. Use good, long lengths of thread for this as the finished plait will be a bit less than half the length of the original thread, and it will give you plenty of time to repeat the spell over and over. The repetition of the spell will be a crucial element in the magic. Use a simple form of words (for example, for a healing spell use the name of the person and the words "be well") and repeat it over and over until you are no longer aware of what you are saying. A plaited cord may be used on its own, or combined with other elements of magical working. It could be used to thread through a holed witchstone or other amulet to add to its power, or as a hanger for one of your house charms. A witch's mirror could be kept safe and secret by wrapping it in a special piece of fabric and tying a plaited cord around it.

When my coven is asked to work magic for someone who is ill, we use a spell which we simply call the Big Red Plait. Lots of lengths of red wool (the more the better), at least five yards (or metres) long tied together at the top are grouped together into three hanks. Everyone then takes it in turn to plait these hanks together, repeating the spell and concentrating our magical wills as we go. It will usually take at least half an hour to do this. When all the wool is plaited the end is tied and the spell is given a final boost. It is then given to the person for whom it has been made.

Knitting can be used for many magical purposes. Cecil Williamson collected a knitting spell in which something the witch wished to be rid of or banish would be repeated over and over whilst the witch knitted using black wool. Cecil used glass knitting needles for this spell, but in my experience any needles will do. When the spell had been repeated to the witch's satisfaction, the wool would be pulled off the needles and burnt. I tried this spell when I first met Cecil many years ago and was amazed at how quickly and effectively it worked.

Whilst knitting a pair of socks for a friend or something for a new baby, I will concentrate my will and knit my good wishes for them as I work. A friend was desperate to find a new place to live. She described to me the kind of house she wanted and I knitted a picture of it, concentrating throughout on her getting what she needed.

Sewing can be used in exactly the same way: stitch your intent into whatever you make.

Spell bags can be assembled using herbs grains, stone and whatever other materials you choose and placed in small drawstring bags which you can easily sew. I like to sew these by hand as I find it increases my concentration; every stitch is done with intent.

These are just some examples of simple spell making which you can adapt and use for your own purposes. They work because they combine repetitive activities with magical will. Like much of the witchcraft I have described here they may seem like simple and perhaps inconsequential activities but, if done with the right attitude, their effects can be profound. Any kind of art or craft or activity which allows you to combine the physical making of something with magical concentration will achieve the same effects. Many of the crafts which I and other witches practise are everyday domestic things which are looked down on by grand folk but which have always been used by witches to work their magic. Cooking, for example is an activity which most of us do most of the time but how often is it done with real magical meaning? Food may be prepared for a magical ritual with concentration on the purpose of the ritual. This works particularly well for magic which celebrates the round of the seasons. I like to make a harvest loaf of bread for Lammas. As I do it I concentrate on the meaning of Lammas and the sacrifice of the God who becomes the bread that we eat. Anything done with the right intent can be a magical act.

In conclusion, I hope that this book has encouraged you to go and make your own witchcraft and to find witchcraft in things which seem on the surface to be simple and perhaps even trivial, but which can lead you deep into the ways of magic. I hope it will inspire you to work witchcraft in a practical and also a deep way. If magic is lived and experienced it becomes a living and a powerful force which will guide and shape your life. Magic will be present in everything that you do with mindful intent, whether it be sitting out and speaking with the spirits, honouring the gods, tying knots in a thread, carving an ash staff or making sloe gin. Hail to the Gods and the spirits. Blessed Be!

Further Reading

The books listed below will be of interest to those readers who wish to delve deeper into some of the subjects mentioned in this book, especially the moon and lunar time, herbalism and folklore.

CROWLEY, Vivianne: *Wicca* (Aquarian Press, Wellingborough, 1989)

EVANS, George Ewart: *The Pattern Under The Plough* (Faber and Faber, London, 1966)

FORTUNE, Dion: *The Sea Priestess* (Aquarian Press edition, Wellingborough, 1989)

HUSON, Paul: *Mastering Witchcraft* (Perigee edition, New York, 1980)

HUSON, Paul: *Mastering Herbalism* (Abacus edition, London, 1977)

HUTTON, Ronald: *The Triumph Of The Moon* (Oxford University Press, 1999)

LACEY, Louise: *Lunaception* (Warner Books, New York, 1976)

REDROVE, Peter and SHUTTLE, Penelope: *The Wise Wound* (Revised Paladin edition, Collins, London, 1986)

ST LEGER GORDON, Ruth: *The Witchcraft And Folklore Of Dartmoor* (Robert Hale, London, 1965)

A selection of other Capall Bann titles:

Shamanic Links - A Comprehensive Foundation For Modern Shamanic Practice by Adam Bear

Woodland structure; animal tracking; identifying trees, conservation, shamanic lore; spiritual healing; auras; making magical tools, totems and power animals; festival, spells and much more - a very practical and magical book. ISBN 186163 301 7   £17.95

HerbCraft - A Guide to the Shamanic and Ritual Use of Herbs
by Susan Lavender and Anna Franklin

"I would highly recommend this publication...a must for your bookshelf" Beltane Fire
"....an excellent and truly comprehensive work, an essential reference and invaluable companion for everyone interested in the use of herbs for magic and ritual. Highly recommended" Prediction
"most comprehensive book...The sheer amount of information in this book is staggering...books with this kind of collated information are rare treasures." Manchester Pagan Wheel

Moves beyond herb folklore and examines their true magical nature, showing how power plants can be employed for the transformation of Self and consciousness, according to the teachings of Native Pagan Tradition. Detailed descriptions of herbs, cultivating them for magical purposes, their traditional uses, explanations of lore, the art of herb simples and traditional recipes. Correspondences - animal totems, magical tools, deities, planets, elements and festivals. Set out in alphabetical order, with appendices designed to help each individual with their own personal development. ISBN 1898307 57 1   £19.95   600 pages

Magical Incenses and Oils by Anna Franklin

Incense; perfumes burned to release fragrant smoke, has been used all over the world from ancient times to the present day. Rising smoke has always been associated with prayer rising to the Gods, whether from the domestic hearth, the Pagan altar, the Druid's needfire or the Catholic church's incense burner. Incenses affect our emotions, subtly induce moods and, on a more profound level, can be used to change the vibration of the atmosphere to the level needed for magical working or healing. This book shows you how to make magical incenses and oils, how to choose suitable ingredients and how to use those incenses and oils to the best effect. Anna Franklin is the co-author of the widely acclaimed 'Herbcraft - Shamanic and Ritual Use of Herbs', and several other titles in this field. ISBN 186163 108 1   £10.95

The Book of Dowsing and Divining by Sue Phillips

MOST PEOPLE CAN DOWSE, it's simply a question of learning how. This book will teach you to find out all kinds of things from health problems to buried treasure; from ley lines to what colour you should wear to enhance your energies. Packed with illustrations, The Book of Dowsing and Divining contains clear step by step instructions for divining with forked twigs, dowsing rods and pendulums. There are easy instructions for making your own dowsing tools, too, even if you have no practical experience or money; and ideas for improvisation when you simply have to dowse, but have left your equipment at home. Sue Phillips is a dowser and healer of many years' experience and has distilled her knowledge to bring you this highly readable and entertaining How-to book. ISBN 186163 1200   £7.95

FREE DETAILED CATALOGUE

Capall Bann is owned and run by people actively involved in many of the areas in which we publish. A detailed illustrated catalogue is available on request, SAE or International Postal Coupon appreciated. **Titles can be ordered direct from Capall Bann,** by post (cheque or PO with order), via our web site **www.capallbann.co.uk** using credit/debit card or Paypal, or from good bookshops and specialist outlets.

A Breath Behind Time, Terri Hector
A Soul is Born by Eleyna Williamson
Angels and Goddesses - Celtic Christianity & Paganism, M. Howard
The Art of Conversation With the Genius Loci, Barry Patterson
Arthur - The Legend Unveiled, C Johnson & E Lung
Astrology The Inner Eye - A Guide in Everyday Language, E Smith
Auguries and Omens - The Magical Lore of Birds, Yvonne Aburrow
Asyniur - Women's Mysteries in the Northern Tradition, S McGrath
Beginnings - Geomancy, Builder's Rites & Electional Astrology in the
     European Tradition, Nigel Pennick
Between Earth and Sky, Julia Day
The Book of Seidr, Runic John
Caer Sidhe - Celtic Astrology and Astronomy, Michael Bayley
Call of the Horned Piper, Nigel Jackson
Can't Sleep, Won't Sleep, Linda Louisa Dell
Carnival of the Animals, Gregor Lamb
Cat's Company, Ann Walker
Celebrating Nature, Gordon MacLellan
Celtic Faery Shamanism, Catrin James
Celtic Faery Shamanism - The Wisdom of the Otherworld, Catrin James
Celtic Lore & Druidic Ritual, Rhiannon Ryall
Celtic Sacrifice - Pre Christian Ritual & Religion, Marion Pearce
Celtic Saints and the Glastonbury Zodiac, Mary Caine
Circle and the Square, Jack Gale
Come Back To Life, Jenny Smedley
Company of Heaven, Jan McDonald
Compleat Vampyre - The Vampyre Shaman, Nigel Jackson
Cottage Witchcraft, Jan McDonald
Creating Form From the Mist - The Wisdom of Women in Celtic Myth and
     Culture, Lynne Sinclair-Wood
Crystal Clear - A Guide to Quartz Crystal, Jennifer Dent
Crystal Doorways, Simon & Sue Lilly

Crossing the Borderlines - Guising, Masking & Ritual Animal Disguise in the
  European Tradition, Nigel Pennick
Dragons of the West, Nigel Pennick
Dreamtime by Linda Louisa Dell
Dreamweaver by Elen Sentier
Earth Dance - A Year of Pagan Rituals, Jan Brodie
Earth Harmony - Places of Power, Holiness & Healing, Nigel Pennick
Earth Magic, Margaret McArthur
Egyptian Animals - Guardians & Gateways of the Gods, Akkadia Ford
Eildon Tree (The) Romany Language & Lore, Michael Hoadley
Enchanted Forest - The Magical Lore of Trees, Yvonne Aburrow
Eternal Priestess, Sage Weston
Eternally Yours Faithfully, Roy Radford & Evelyn Gregory
Everything You Always Wanted To Know About Your Body, But So Far
  Nobody's Been Able To Tell You, Chris Thomas & D Baker
Experiencing the Green Man, Rob Hardy & Teresa Moorey
Face of the Deep - Healing Body & Soul, Penny Allen
Fairies and Nature Spirits, Teresa Moorey
Fairies in the Irish Tradition, Molly Gowen
Familiars - Animal Powers of Britain, Anna Franklin
Flower Wisdom, Katherine Kear
Fool's First Steps, (The) Chris Thomas
Forest Paths - Tree Divination, Brian Harrison, Ill. S. Rouse
From Past to Future Life, Dr Roger Webber
From Stagecraft To Witchcraft, Patricia Crowther
Gardening For Wildlife Ron Wilson
God Year, The, Nigel Pennick & Helen Field
Goddess on the Cross, Dr George Young
Goddess Year, The, Nigel Pennick & Helen Field
Goddesses, Guardians & Groves, Jack Gale
Handbook For Pagan Healers, Liz Joan
Handbook of Fairies, Ronan Coghlan
Healing Book, The, Chris Thomas and Diane Baker
Healing Homes, Jennifer Dent
Healing Journeys, Paul Williamson
Healing Stones, Sue Philips
Heathen Paths - Viking and Anglo Saxon Beliefs by Pete Jennings
Herb Craft - Shamanic & Ritual Use of Herbs, Lavender & Franklin
Hidden Heritage - Exploring Ancient Essex, Terry Johnson
Hub of the Wheel, Skytoucher
In and Out the Windows, Dilys Gator
In Search of Herne the Hunter, Eric Fitch
In Search of the Green Man, Peter Hill
Inner Celtia, Alan Richardson & David Annwn
Inner Mysteries of the Goths, Nigel Pennick
Inner Space Workbook - Develop Through Tarot, Cat Summers & Julian Vayne

In Search of Pagan Gods, Teresa Moorey
Intuitive Journey, Ann Walker Isis - African Queen, Akkadia Ford
Journey Home, The, Chris Thomas
Kecks, Keddles & Kesh - Celtic Lang & The Cog Almanac, Bayley
Language of the Psycards, Berenice
Legend of Robin Hood, The, Richard Rutherford-Moore
Lid Off the Cauldron, Patricia Crowther
Light From the Shadows - Modern Traditional Witchcraft, Gwyn
Living Tarot, Ann Walker
Lore of the Sacred Horse, Marion Davies
Lost Lands & Sunken Cities (2nd ed.), Nigel Pennick
Lyblác, Anglo Saxon Witchcraft by Wulfeage
The Magic and Mystery of Trees, Teresa Moorey
Magic For the Next 1,000 Years, Jack Gale
Magic of Herbs - A Complete Home Herbal, Rhiannon Ryall
Magical Guardians - Exploring the Spirit and Nature of Trees, Philip Heselton
Magical History of the Horse, Janet Farrar & Virginia Russell
Magical Lore of Animals, Yvonne Aburrow
Magical Lore of Cats, Marion Davies
Magical Lore of Herbs, Marion Davies
The Magical Properties of Plants - and How to Find Them by Tylluan Penry
Magick Without Peers, Ariadne Rainbird & David Rankine
Masks of Misrule - Horned God & His Cult in Europe, Nigel Jackson
Medicine For The Coming Age, Lisa Sand MD
Medium Rare - Reminiscences of a Clairvoyant, Muriel Renard
Menopausal Woman on the Run, Jaki da Costa
Mind Massage - 60 Creative Visualisations, Marlene Maundrill
Mirrors of Magic - Evoking the Spirit of the Dewponds, P Heselton
The Moon and You, Teresa Moorey
Moon Mysteries, Jan Brodie
Mysteries of the Runes, Michael Howard
Mystic Life of Animals, Ann Walker
New Celtic Oracle The, Nigel Pennick & Nigel Jackson
Oracle of Geomancy, Nigel Pennick
Pagan Feasts - Seasonal Food for the 8 Festivals, Franklin & Phillips
Paganism For Teens, Jess Wynne
Patchwork of Magic - Living in a Pagan World, Julia Day
Pathworking - A Practical Book of Guided Meditations, Pete Jennings
Personal Power, Anna Franklin
Pickingill Papers - The Origins of Gardnerian Wicca, Bill Liddell
Pillars of Tubal Cain, Nigel Jackson
Places of Pilgrimage and Healing, Adrian Cooper
Planet Earth - The Universe's Experiment, Chris Thomas
Practical Divining, Richard Foord
Practical Meditation, Steve Hounsome
Practical Spirituality, Steve Hounsome

Psychic Self Defence - Real Solutions, Jan Brodie
Real Fairies, David Tame
Reality - How It Works & Why It Mostly Doesn't, Rik Dent
Romany Tapestry, Michael Houghton
Runic Astrology, Nigel Pennick
Sacred Animals, Gordon MacLellan
Sacred Celtic Animals, Marion Davies, Ill. Simon Rouse
Sacred Dorset - On the Path of the Dragon, Peter Knight
Sacred Grove - The Mysteries of the Forest, Yvonne Aburrow
Sacred Geometry, Nigel Pennick
Sacred Nature, Ancient Wisdom & Modern Meanings, A Cooper
Sacred Ring - Pagan Origins of British Folk Festivals, M. Howard
Season of Sorcery - On Becoming a Wisewoman, Poppy Palin
Seasonal Magic - Diary of a Village Witch, Paddy Slade
Secret Places of the Goddess, Philip Heselton
Secret Signs & Sigils, Nigel Pennick
The Secrets of East Anglian Magic, Nigel Pennick
A Seeker's Guide To Past Lives, Paul Williamson
Seeking Pagan Gods, Teresa Moorey
A Seer's Guide To Crystal Divination, Gale Halloran
Self Enlightenment, Mayan O'Brien
Soul Resurgence, Poppy Palin
Spirits of the Air, Jaq D Hawkins
Spirits of the Water, Jaq D Hawkins
Spirits of the Fire, Jaq D Hawkins
Spirits of the Aether, Jaq D Hawkins
Spirits of the Earth, Jaq D Hawkins
Stony Gaze, Investigating Celtic Heads John Billingsley
Stumbling Through the Undergrowth , Mark Kirwan-Heyhoe
Subterranean Kingdom, The, revised 2nd ed, Nigel Pennick
Symbols of Ancient Gods, Rhiannon Ryall
Talking to the Earth, Gordon MacLellan
Talking With Nature, Julie Hood
Taming the Wolf - Full Moon Meditations, Steve Hounsome
Teachings of the Wisewomen, Rhiannon Ryall
The Other Kingdoms Speak, Helena Hawley
Transformation of Housework, Ben Bushill
Treading the Mill - Practical CraftWorking in Modern Traditional Witchcraft by Nigel
Pearson
Tree: Essence of Healing, Simon & Sue Lilly
Tree: Essence, Spirit & Teacher, Simon & Sue Lilly
Tree Seer, Simon & Sue Lilly
Torch and the Spear, Patrick Regan
Understanding Chaos Magic, Jaq D Hawkins
Understanding Second Sight, Dilys Gater
Understanding Spirit Guides, Dilys Gater

Understanding Star Children, Dilys Gater
The Urban Shaman, Dilys Gater
Vortex - The End of History, Mary Russell
Walking the Tides - Seasonal Rhythms and Traditional Lore in Natural Craft by Nigel Pearson
Warp and Weft - In Search of the I-Ching, William de Fancourt
Warriors at the Edge of Time, Jan Fry
Water Witches, Tony Steele
Way of the Magus, Michael Howard
Weaving a Web of Magic, Rhiannon Ryall
West Country Wicca, Rhiannon Ryall
What's Your Poison? vol 1, Tina Tarrant
Wheel of the Year, Teresa Moorey & Jane Brideson
Wildwitch - The Craft of the Natural Psychic, Poppy Palin
Wildwood King , Philip Kane
A Wisewoman's Book of Tea Leaf Reading, Pat Barki
The Witching Path, Moira Stirland
The Witch's Kitchen, Val Thomas
The Witches' Heart, Eileen Smith
Witches of Oz, Matthew & Julia Philips
Witchcraft Myth Magic Mystery and... Not Forgetting Fairies, Ralph Harvey
Wondrous Land - The Faery Faith of Ireland by Dr Kay Mullin
Working With Crystals, Shirley o'Donoghue
Working With Natural Energy, Shirley o'Donoghue
Working With the Merlin, Geoff Hughes
Your Talking Pet, Ann Walker
The Zodiac Experience, Patricia Crowther

FREE detailed catalogue
Contact: Capall Bann Publishing, Auton Farm, Milverton, Somerset, TA4 1NE
www.capallbann.co.uk